COLONIAL DAYS

IN

OLD NEW YORK

Colonial Days in Old New York

Alice Morse Earle

HERITAGE BOOKS
2011

HERITAGE BOOKS
AN IMPRINT OF HERITAGE BOOKS, INC.

Books, CDs, and more—Worldwide

For our listing of thousands of titles see our website
at
www.HeritageBooks.com

A Facsimile Reprint
Published 2011 by
HERITAGE BOOKS, INC.
Publishing Division
100 Railroad Ave. #104
Westminster, Maryland 21157

Copyright © 1896 Charles Scribner's Sons

— Publisher's Notice —
In reprints such as this, it is often not possible to remove blemishes from the original. We feel the contents of this book warrant its reissue despite these blemishes and hope you will agree and read it with pleasure.

International Standard Book Numbers
Paperbound: 978-1-55613-368-8
Clothbound: 978-0-7884-8612-8

TO

THE SOCIETY OF COLONIAL DAMES
OF THE
STATE OF NEW YORK

THIS BOOK IS DEDICATED BY A LOYAL
AND LOVING MEMBER

THE AUTHOR

PREFACE

This book should perhaps have been "intituled" Colonial Days in New Netherland, for much of the life described herein was in the days of Dutch rule. But it was New Netherland for scarce half a century, and the name is half-forgotten, though it remained, both in outer life and in heart, a Dutch colonie, even when the province was New York and an English governor had control. In New Netherland, as in every place where the Dutch plant a colony, as in South Africa to-day, Dutch ways, Dutch notions, the Dutch tongue lingered long. To this day, Dutch influence and Dutch traits, as well as Dutch names, are ever present and are a force in New York life.

Fair and beautiful lay the broad harbor centuries ago before the eyes of Hendrick Hudson and his sea-weary men; a "pleasant place" was Manhattan; "'t lange eylandt was the

PREFACE

pearl of New Nederland;" the noble river, the fertile shores, all seemed to the discoverers and to the early colonists to smile a welcome and a promise of happy homes. Still to-day the bay, the islands, the river, the shores welcome with the same promise. In grateful thanks for that welcome and for the fulfilment of that promise of old, — for more years of life in New York than were spent in my birthplace in New England, — and in warm affection for my many friends of Dutch descent, have I — to use the words of Rabelais — "adjoined these words and testimony for the honour I bear to antiquity."

ALICE MORSE EARLE.

Brooklyn Heights,
    September, 1896.

CONTENTS

CHAPTER		PAGE
I.	THE LIFE OF A DAY	1
II.	EDUCATION AND CHILD-LIFE	14
III.	WOOING AND WEDDING	45
IV.	TOWN LIFE	70
V.	DUTCH TOWN HOMES	98
VI.	DUTCH FARMHOUSES	115
VII.	THE DUTCH LARDER	128
VIII.	THE DUTCH VROUWS	154
IX.	THE COLONIAL WARDROBE	172
X.	HOLIDAYS	185
XI.	AMUSEMENTS AND SPORTS	204
XII.	CRIMES AND PUNISHMENTS	227
XIII.	CHURCH AND SUNDAY IN OLD NEW YORK	261
XIV.	"THE END OF HIS DAYS"	293

COLONIAL DAYS
IN
OLD NEW YORK

CHAPTER I

THE LIFE OF A DAY

At the first break of day, every spring and summer morn, the quiet Dutch sleepers in the old colonial town of Albany were roused by three loud blasts of a horn sounded far and wide by a sturdy cow-herd; and from street and dooryard came in quick answer the jingle-jangle, the klingle-klangle of scores of loud-tongued brass and iron bells which hung from the necks of steady-going hungry Dutch cows who followed the town-herder forth, each day to pastures green.

On the broad town-commons or the fertile river-meadows Uldrick Heyn and his "chosen proper youngster," his legally appointed aid, watched faithfully all day long their neighbors' cattle; and as honest herdsmen earned well their sea-want and their handsel of butter,[1] dallying not in tavern, and drinking not of wine, as they were sternly forbidden by the *schepens*, until when early dews were falling they quit their meadow grasses mellow, for " at a quarter of an hour before the sun goes down the cattle shall be delivered at the church." Thence the patient kine slowly wandered or were driven each to her own home-stall, her protecting cow-shed.

In New Amsterdam the town's cow-herd was Gabriel Carpsey; and when his day's work was done, he walked at sunset through the narrow lanes and streets of the little settlement, sounding at each dooryard Gabriel's horn, a warning note of safe return and milking-time.

Until mid-November did the morning cow-horn waken the burghers and their *vrouws* at sunrise; and when with cold winter the horn lay silent, they must have sorely missed their unfailing eye-opener.

Scarce had the last cow departed in the early morn from her master's dooryard, before there rose in the gray light from each vast-throated chimney throughout the little town a faint line of pale, wavering smoke blown up in increasing puffs with skilful bellows from last night's brands upon the hearth. And quickly the slender line of smoke grew and grew to a great cloud over each steep-roofed house, and soon with the smell of the burning brush and light pine that were coaxing into hot flames the sturdy oak back and fore logs, were borne forth also appetizing odors of breakfast to greet the early morn, telling of each thrifty *huys-vrouw* who within the walls of her cheerful kitchen was cooking a good solid Dutch breakfast for her *mann.*

Cans of buttermilk or good beer, brewed perhaps by the patroon, washed down this breakfast of suppawn and rye-bread and grated cheese and sausage or head-cheese; beer there was in plenty, in ankers, even in tuns, in every household. Soon *mynheer* filled his long pipe with native tobacco, and departed with much deliberation of movement; a sturdy, honest figure, of decent carriage, neatly and soberly and warmly clad, with thrift and prosperity and contentment showing in every curve of his too-well-rounded figure. Adown the narrow street he paused to trade in peltries or lumber, if he were middle-aged and well-to-do; and were he sturdy and young, he threshed grain on the barn-floor, or ground corn at the windmill, or felled wood on the hillside; or perchance, were he old or young, he fished in the river all day long,— a truly dignified day's work, meet for any sober citizen, one requiring much judgment and ski'l and reflection.

And as he fished, again he smoked, and ever he smoked. "The Dutch are obstinate and incessant smokers," chronicles the English clergyman Wolley, Chaplain of Fort James, New York, in 1678, "whose diet, especially of the boorish sort, being sallets and brawn and very often picked buttermilk, require the use of that herb to keep their phlegm from coagulating and curdling." The word "boorish" was not a term of reproach, nor was the frequent appellation "Dutch bore," over which some historians of the colony have seen fit to make merry, both boor and bore meaning simply *boer*, or farmer. "Knave meant once no more than lad; villain than peasant; a boor was only a farmer; a varlet was but a serving-man; a churl but a strong fellow."

What fishing was to the goodman of the

house, knitting was to the goodwife, — a soothing, monotonous occupation, ever at hand, ever welcome, ever useful. Why, the family could scarce be clothed in comfort without these clicking needles! A goodly supply of well-knit, carefully dyed stockings was the housekeeper's pride; and well they might be, for little were they hidden. The full knee-breeches of father and son displayed above the buckled shoes a long expanse of sturdy hosiery, and the short petticoats of mother and daughter did not hide the scarlet clocks of their own making. From the moment when the farmer gave the fleece of the sheep into the hands of his women-kind, every step of its transformation into stockings (except the knitting) was so tiresome and tedious that it is wearying even to read of it, — cleaning, washing, dyeing, carding, greasing, rolling, spinning, winding, rinsing, knotting, — truly might the light, tidy, easy knitting seem a pastime.

The endless round of "domesticall kind of drudgeries that women are put to," as Howell says, would prove a very full list when made out from the life of one of these colonial housewives. It seems to us, of modern

COLONIAL DAYS

labor-saved and drudgery-void days, a truly overwhelming list; but the Dutch *huysvrouw* did not stagger under the burden, nor shrink from it, nor, indeed, did she deem any of her daily work drudgery. The sense of thrift, of plenty, of capability, of satisfaction, was so strong as to overcome the distaste to the labor of production.

She had as a recreation, a delight, the care of

> "A garden through whose latticed gates
> The imprisoned pinks and tulips gazed,"

a trim, stiff little garden, which often graced the narrow front dooryard; a garden perhaps of a single flower-bed surrounded by aromatic herbs for medicinal and culinary use, but homelike and beloved as such gardens ever are, and specially beloved as such gardens are by the Dutch. Many were the tulip bulbs and "coronation" pink roots that had been brought or sent over from Holland, and were affectionately cherished as reminders of the far-away Fatherland. The enthusiastic traveller Van der Donck wrote that by 1653 Netherlanders had already blooming in their American garden-borders "white and red roses, stock roses, cornelian roses, eglantine, jenoffelins, gillyflowers, different varieties of fine tulips, crown-imperials, white lilies, anemones, bare-dames, violets, marigolds, summersots, clove-trees." Garden-flowers of native growth were "sunflowers, red and yellow lilies, morning-stars, bell-flowers, red and white and yellow maritoffles." I do not know what all these "flower-gentles" were, but surely it was no dull array of blossoms; nor were their glories dimmed because they opened ever by the side of the homely cabbages and lettuce, the humble cucumbers and beans, that were equally beloved and tended by the garden-maker.

And the housewife had her beloved and homelike poultry. Flocks of snowy geese went waddling slowly down the town streets, seeking the water-side; giving rich promise of fat holiday dinners and plumper and more plentiful feather-beds; comfortable and thriving looking as geese always are, and ever indicative of prosperous, thrifty homes, they comported well with the pipe-smoking burgher and his knitting *huys-vrouw* and their homelike dwelling.

There was one element of beauty and

picturesqueness which idealized the little town and gave it an added element of life, —

> " Over all and everywhere
> The sails of windmills sink and soar
> Like wings of sea-gulls on the shore."

The beauty of the windmills probably was not so endearing to the settlers as their homelikeness. They made the new strange land and the new little towns seem like the Fatherland. The Indians greatly feared them; as one chronicler states, "they durst not come near their long arms and big teeth biting the corn in pieces." Last, and not least in the minds of the thrifty Dutch, the windmills helped to turn to profit the rich harvests of grain which were the true foundation of the colony's prosperity, — not the rich peltries of beaver, as was at first boastfully vaunted by the fur-traders.

As the day wore on, the day's work was ended, and a neighborly consultation and exchange of greetings formed the day's recreation. The burgher went to the little market-house, and with his neighbors and a few chance travellers, such as the skippers on the river-sloops, he smoked again his long pipe and talked over the weighty affairs of the *colonie*. In the summer-time goodman and goodwife both went from stoop to stoop of the close-gathered houses, for a *klappernye*, or chat all together. This was a feature of the colony, architectural and social, and noted by all travellers, — "the benches at the door, on which the old carls sit and smoke." Here the goodwife recounted the simple events of the day, — the number of skeins of yarn she had spun; the yards of linen she had woven; the doings of the dye-pot; the crankiness of the churning, to which she had sung her churning charm, —

> "Buitterchee, buitterchee, comm
> Alican laidlechee tubichee vall."

Perhaps she told her *commeres*, her gossips, of a fresh suspicion of a betrothal, or perhaps sad news of a sick neighbor or a funeral. This was never scandal, for each one's affairs were every one's affairs; in the weal or woe of one the whole community joined, and in many of the influences or effects of that weal or woe all had a part. It was noted by historians that the Dutch were most open in discussion of all the doings of the community, and had no dread of publicity of every-day life.

COLONIAL DAYS

Of this habit of colonial neighborliness, Mrs. Anne Grant wrote in her "Memoir of an American Lady"—Madam Schuyler—from contemporary knowledge of early life in Albany:—

"The life of new settlers in a situation like this, when the very foundations of society were to be laid, was a life of exigencies. Every individual took an interest in the general welfare, and contributed their respective shares of intelligence and sagacity to aid plans that embraced important objects relative to the common good. This community seemed to have a common stock, not only of sufferings and enjoyments, but of information and ideas."

When the sun was setting and the cows came home, the family gathered on stools and forms around the well-supplied board, and a plentiful supper of suppawn and milk and a sallet filled the hungry mouths, and was eaten from wooden trenchers and pewter porringers with pewter or silver spoons. The night had come; here were shelter and a warm hearthstone, and, though in the new wild world, it was in truth a home.

Sometimes, silently smoking with the man of the house, there sat in the winter *schemerlicht*, the shadow-light or gloaming, around the great glowing hearth, a group of dusky picturesque forms, — friendly Mohawks, who, when their furs were safely sold, could be welcomed, and were ever tolerated and harbored by the kindly Swannekins; and as the shadows gathered into the "fore-night," and the fierce wind screamed down the great chimney and drew out into the darkness long tongues of orange and scarlet flames from the oak and hickory fires (burning, says one early traveller, half up the chimney), there was homely comfort within, and peace in the white man's wigwam.

> "What matter how the North-wind raved, —
> Blow high, blow low, not all its snow
> Could quench that hearth-fire's ruddy glow."

And the blanketed squaw felt in her savage breast the spirit of that home, and gently nursed her swaddled pappoose; and the silent *Wilden*, ever smoking, listened to the Dutch *huys-moeder*, who, undressing little Hybertje and Jan and Goosje for their long night's sleep, sang to them the nursery song of the Hollanders, of the Fatherland: —

> "Trip a troup a tronjes,
> De vaarken in de boonjes,

> De koejes in de klaver,
> De paarden in de haver,
> De kalver in de lang gras,
> De eenjes in de water plas,
> So groot myn klein poppetje was."

Or if it were mid-December, the children sang to Kriss-Kringle: —

> "Saint Nicholaes, goed heilig man,
> Trekt uw' besten tabbard aan,
> En reist daamee naar Amsterdam,
> Von Amsterdam naar Spange,
> Waar Appellen von Orange
> En Appellen von Granaten
> Rollen door de straaten.
>
> "Saint Nicholaes, myn goeden vriend,
> Ik heb uwe altyd wel gediend,
> Als gy my nu wat wilt geben
> Zal ik un dienen als myn leben."

Then the warming-pan was filled with hot coals, and thrust warily between the ice-cold sheets of the children's beds, and perhaps they were given a drink of mulled cider or simmering beer; and scarcely were they sleeping in their warm flannel *cosyntjes*, or nightcaps with long capes, when the curfew rang out from the church belfry. It was eight o'clock, — *'t Is tijdt te bedde te gaen*. The housewife carefully covered "the dull red brands with ashes over" for the fire of the morrow, and went to bed. The "tap-toes" sounded from the fort, and every house was silent.

And as the honest *mynheer* and his good *vrouw* slept warmly in their fireside alcove, and softly between their great feather-beds, so they also slept serenely; for they were not left unprotected from marauding Indian or Christian, nor unwatched by the ever-thoughtful town authorities. Through the little town marched boldly every night a sturdy *kloppermann*, or rattle-watch, with strong staff and brass-bound hourglass and lighted lanthorn; and, best of all, he bore a large *klopper*, or rattle, which he shook loudly and reassuringly at each door all through the dark hours of the night, "from nine o'clock to break of the day," to warn both housekeepers and thieves that he was near at hand; and as was bidden by the worshipful *schepens*, he called out what o'clock, and what weather; — and thus guarded, let us leave them sleeping, these honest Dutch home-folk, as they have now slept for centuries in death, waiting to hear called out to them with clear voice "at break of the day" from another world, "A fair morning, and all's well."

CHAPTER II

EDUCATION AND CHILD-LIFE

As soon as the little American baby was born in New Netherland, he was taken to the church by his Dutch papa, and with due array of sponsors was christened by the domine from the *doop-becken*, or dipping-bowl, in the Dutch Reformed Church. New Yorkers had a beautiful silver *doop-becken* in 1695, and the church on the corner of Thirty-Eighth Street and Madison Avenue has it still. It was made in Amsterdam from silver coin and ornaments brought by the good folk of the Garden Street Church as offerings. For it Domine Henricus Selyns, "of nimble faculty," then minister of that church, and formerly of Breuckelen, and the first poet of Brooklyn, wrote these pious and graceful verses, which were inscribed on the bowl:

"Op't blote water stelt geen hoot
'T was beter noyt gebooren.

IN OLD NEW YORK

    Maer, ziet iets meerder in de Dorp
      Zo' gaet nien noÿt verlooren.
    Hoe Christús met sÿn dierbaer Bloedt
      Mÿ reÿniglt van myn Zonden.
    En door syn Geest mÿ leven doet
      En wast mÿn Vuÿle Wonden."

Which translated reads: —

"Do not put your hope in simple water alone, 't were better never to be born.
But behold something more in baptism, for that will prevent your getting lost.
How Christ's precious blood cleanses me of my sins,
And now I may live through His spirit and be cleansed of my vile wounds."

This christening was the sole social or marked event of the *kindeken's* infancy, and little else do we know of his early life. He ate and slept, as do all infants. In cradles slept these children of the Dutch, — deep-hooded cradles to protect from the chill draughts of the poorly heated houses. In cradles of birch bark the Albany babies slept; and pretty it was to see the fat little Dutchmen sleeping in those wildwood tributes of the Indian mothers' skill to the children of the men who had driven the children of the redmen from their homes.

Children were respectful, almost cowed,

in their bearing to their parents, and were enjoined by ministers and magistrates to filial obedience. When the government left the Dutch control and became English, the Calvinistic sternness of laws as to obedience to parents in maturer years which was seen in New England was also found in New York.

"If any Child or Children, above sixteen years of age, and of Sufficient understanding, shall smite their Natural Father or Mother, unless provoked and forct for their selfe preservation from Death or Mayming, at the Complaint of the said Father or Mother, and not otherwise, they being Sufficient witness thereof, that Child, or those Children so offending shall be put to Death."

A few prim little letters of English children have survived the wear and tear of years, and still show us in their pretty wording the formal and respectful language of the times. Martha Bockée Flint, in that interesting and valuable book, "Early Long Island," gives this letter written to Major Ephenetus Platt "at Huntting-town" by a little girl eleven years old: —

EVER HONORED GRANDFATHER;
SIR: My long absence from you and my dear Grandmother has been not a little tedious to me.

IN OLD NEW YORK

But what renders me a Vast Deal of pleasure is Being intensely happy with a Dear and Tender Mother-in-Law and frequent oppertunities of hearing of your Health and Welfair which I pray God may long Continue. What I have more to add is to acquaint you that I have already made a Considerable Progress in Learning. I have already gone through some Rules of Arithmetic, and in a little Time shall be able of giving you a Better acct of my Learning, and in mean time I am Duty Bound to subscribe myself

    Your most obedient and
      Duty full Granddaughter
        PEGGA TREADWELL.

In the Lloyd Collections is a charming little letter from another Long Island miss, ten years of age. The penmanship is elegant and finished, as was that of her elders at that date.

We have, however, scant sources from which to learn of the life of children in colonial New York. No diarist of Pepysian minuteness tells of the children of New Netherland as does the faithful Samuel Sewall of those of New England; no collections of letters such as the Winthrop Papers and others recount the various items of domestic life. There are none of the pious and gar-

COLONIAL DAYS

rulous writings of ministers such as Cotton Mather, who in diary and various literary compositions give another side of their life. We have no such messages from the colonial Dutch. In whatever depended on the use of "a flourit pen," posterity is neither richer nor wiser for the Dutch settlers having lived. Nor were their English successors much fonder of literary composition. Nothing but formal records of churches, of courts, of business life, offer to us any pages for study and drawing of inference. And from these records the next hint of the life of these colonial children, sad to relate, is to their discredit. The pragmatic magistrates kept up a steady prying and bullying over them. In New Orange, in 1673, "if any children be caught on the street playing, racing, and shouting previous to the termination of the last preaching, the officers of justice may take their hat or upper garment, which shall not be restored to the parents until they have paid a fine of two guilders," which, we may be sure, would insure the miserable infants summary punishment on arriving home.

Matters were no better in New Amsterdam. One amusing complaint was brought up against "ye wretched boys" of that settlement, and by one high in authority, Schout De Sille. One of his duties was to patrol the town of New Amsterdam at night to see that all was peaceful as befitted a town which was the daughter of the Dutch government. But the poor *schout* did not find his evening stroll altogether a happy one. He complained that the dogs set upon him, and that tantalizing boys shouted out "The Indians!" at him from behind trees and fences, — which must have startled him sorely, and have been most unpleasantly suggestive in those days of Indian horrors; and his chief complaint was that there was "much cutting of hoekies" by the boys, — which means, I fancy, playing of tricks, of jokes, of *hoaxes*, such as were played on Hock-day in England, or perhaps "playing hookey," as American boys of to-day have been known to do.

As years passed on, I fear some of these young Dutch-Americans were sad rogues. They sore roused the wrath of Albany legislators, as is hereby proven: —

"Whereas ye children of ye s^d city do very unorderly to ye shame and scandall of their parents ryde down ye hills in ye streets of the s^d city with small and great slees on the lord day and in the week by which many accidents may come, now for pventing ye same it is hereby publishd and declard y^t it shall and may be lawful for any Constable in this City or any other person or persons to take any slee or slees from all and every such boys and girls rydeing or offering to ryde down any hill within ye s^d city and breake any slee or slees in pieces. Given under our hands and seals in Albany ye 22th of December in 12th year of Her Maj's reign Anno Domini 1713."

In 1728 Albany boys and girls still were hectored, still were fined by the bullying Albany constable for sliding down the alluringly steep Albany streets on "sleds, small boards, or otherwise."

Mrs. Grant, writing of about the year 1765, speaks of the custom of coasting, but not of the legislation against it, and gives a really delightful picture of coasting-joys, which apparently were then partaken of only by boys. The *schepens* and their successors the constables, joy-destroying Sivas, had evidently succeeded in wresting this pleasure from the girls.

" In town all the boys were extravagantly fond of a diversion that to us would appear a very odd and childish one. The great street of the town sloped down from the hill on which the fort stood, towards the river; between the buildings was an unpaved carriage-road, the foot-path beside the houses being the only part of the street which was paved. In winter the sloping descent, continued for more than a quarter of a mile, acquired firmness from the frost, and became very slippery. Then the amusement commenced. Every boy and youth in town, from eight to eighteen, had a little low sledge, made with a rope like a bridle to the front, by which it could be dragged after one by the hand. On this one or two at most could sit, and this sloping descent being made as smooth as a looking-glass, by sliders' sledges, etc., perhaps a hundred at once set out from the top of this street, each seated in his little sledge with the rope in his hand, which, drawn to the right or left, served to guide him. He pushed it off with a little stick, as one would launch a boat; and then, with the most astonishing velocity, precipitated by the weight of the owner, the little machine glided past, and was at the lower end of the street in an instant. What could be so delightful in this rapid and smooth descent I could never discover; though in a more retired place, and on a smaller scale, I have tried the amusement; but to a young Albanian, sleighing, as he called it, was one of the first joys of life, though attended by the drawback of walking to the top of the declivity, dragging his sledge every time he renewed his flight, for such it might well be called. In the managing this little machine some dexterity was necessary: an unskilful Phaeton was sure to fall. The conveyance was so low that a fall was attended with little danger, yet with much disgrace, for an universal laugh from all sides assailed the fallen charioteer. This laugh was from a very full chorus, for the constant and rapid succession of this procession, where every one had a brother, lover, or kinsman, brought all the young people in town to the porticos, where they used to sit wrapt in furs till ten or eleven at night, engrossed by this delectable spectacle. I have known an Albanian, after residing some years in Britain, and becoming a polished fine gentleman, join the sport and slide down with the rest."

Mrs. Grant tells of another interesting and unusual custom of the children of Albany:

"The children of the town were divided into companies, as they called them, from five to six years of age, until they became marriageable. How those companies first originated, or what were their exact regulations, I cannot say; though I, belonging to none, occasionally mixed with several, yet always as a stranger, notwithstanding that I spoke their current language fluently. Every company contained as many boys as girls. But I do not know that there was any limited number; only this I recollect, that a boy and girl of each company, who were older, cleverer, or had some other preeminence among the rest were called heads of the company, and as such were obeyed by the others.

... Children of different ages in the same family belonged to different companies. Each company at a certain time of the year went in a body to gather a particular kind of berries to the hill. It was a sort of annual festival attended with religious punctuality. Every company had a uniform for this purpose; that is to say, very pretty light baskets made by the Indians, with lids and handles, which hung over one arm, and were adorned with various colors. Every child was permitted to entertain the whole company on its birthday, and once besides, during winter and spring. The master and mistress of the family always were bound to go from home on these occasions, while some old domestic was left to attend and watch over them, with an ample provision of tea, chocolate, preserved and dried fruits, nuts and cakes of various kinds, to which was added cider or a syllabub; for these young friends met at four and amused themselves with the utmost gayety and freedom in any way their fancy dictated."

From all the hints and facts which I have obtained, through letters, diaries, church and court records, of child-life in any of the colonies or provinces among English, German, Swedish, or Dutch settlers, I am sure these Albany young folk were the most favored of their time. I find no signs of such freedom in any other town.

COLONIAL DAYS

It has been asserted that in every town in New York which was settled under the Dutch, a school was established which was taught by a competent teacher who received a small salary from the government, in addition to his other emoluments; and that after the reign of the English, begun in 1664, this public salary ceased, and many of the towns were schoolless.

This statement is not confirmed by a letter of Domine Megapolensis written from Albany in 1657. He says plainly that only Manhattan, Beverwyck, and Fort Casimir had schoolmasters, and he predicts, as a result, "ignorance, a ruined youth, and bewilderment of men's minds." Other authorities, such as Mr. Teunis G. Bergen, state that this liberality where it existed should be accredited to the Dutch church, not the Dutch state, or Dutch West India Company. In truth, it was all one matter. The church was an essential power in the government of New Netherland, as it was in Holland; hence the West India Company and the Classis of Amsterdam conjoined in sending domines with the supply of burgomasters, and likewise furnished school-teachers.

IN OLD NEW YORK

When Wouter van Twiller arrived in 1633 with the first military garrison for New Amsterdam, he brought also envoys of religion and learning, — Domine Everardus Bogardus and the first pedagogue, Adam Roelandsen. Master Roelandsen had a schoolroom assigned to him, and he taught the youthful New Amsterdamites for six years, when he resigned his position, and was banished from the town and went up the river to Renssellaerwyck. I fear he was not a very reputable fellow, "people did not speak well of him;" and he in turn was sued for slander; and some really sad scandals were told about him, both in and out of court. And some folk have also made very merry over the fact that he took in washing, which was really one of the best things we know about him, for it was not at all a disreputable nor unmanly calling in those times. It doubtless proved a very satisfactory source of augmentation of the wavering school-salary, in those days of vast quarterly or semi-annual washings and great *bleeckeryen*, or laundries, — which his probably was, since his bills were paid by the year.

A carpenter, Jan Cornelissen, tired of his

tools and trade, left Rensselaerwyck upon hearing of the vacant teacher's chair in New Amsterdam, went down the river to Manhattan, and in turn taught the school for ten years. Jan was scarcely more reputable than Adam. He lay drunk for a month at a time, and was incorrigibly lazy, — so aggravated Albanians wrote of him. But any one was good enough to teach school. Neither Jan nor Adam was, however, a convicted and banished felon, as were many Virginian schoolmasters.

This drunken schoolmaster was only the first of many. Until this century, the bane of pedagogy in New York was rum. A chorus of colonial schoolmasters could sing, in the words of Goldsmith, —

> " Let schoolmasters puzzle their brains
> With grammar and nonsense and learning;
> Good liquor I stoutly maintain
> Gives genius a better discerning."

Occasionally a certain schoolmaster would be specified in a school-circular as a sober man; proving by the mentioning the infrequency of the qualification.

As the colony grew, other teachers were needed. Governor Stuyvesant sent to the

Classis of Amsterdam for "a pious, well-qualified, and diligent schoolmaster." William Vestens crossed the ocean in answer to this appeal, and taught for five years in one room in New York; while Jan de la Montagne, with an annual salary of two hundred florins, taught at the Harberg — later the Stadt-Huys — and occupied the position of the first public-school teacher.

For years a project of building a schoolhouse was afloat. A spot had been fixed upon, and some money subscribed. In 1649 the Commonalty represented to the West India Company that "the plate was a long time passed around for a common school which has been built with words, for as yet the first stone is not laid." In response to this appeal, a schoolhouse was at last erected. Still another school was opened by Master Hoboocken, who taught in the Governors' bowery, where Dutch-American children were already beginning to throng the green lanes and by-ways. He was succeeded by Evert Pietersen, who was engaged as "Consoler of the Sick, Chorister and Schoolmaster;" and all persons without distinction were ordered not to molest, disturb, or ridicule him in either of these offices, but to "deliver him from every painful sensation." Many of the other schoolmasters had filled similar offices in the church and community.

This public school, maintained with such difficulty and so many rebuffs through these early days, was successfully continued by the Collegiate Dutch Church after the English possession of New York; and it still exists and flourishes, as does the church. This should be a matter of civic pride to every New Yorker. The history of that school has been carefully written, and is most interesting to read.

Many other teachers were licensed to give private lessons, but these public and private schools did not satisfy ambitious New Yorkers. A strong longing was felt in New Amsterdam for a Latin School. A characteristic petition was sent by the burgomasters and *schepens* to the West India Company:

"It is represented that the youth of this place and the neighborhood are increasing in number gradually, and that most of them can read and write, but that some of the citizens and inhabitants would like to send their children to a school the principal of which understands Latin, but are not able to do so without sending them to New England; furthermore, they have not the means to hire a Latin schoolmaster expressly for themselves from New England, and therefore they ask that the West India Company will send out a fit person as Latin schoolmaster, not doubting that the number of persons who will send their children to such a teacher will from year to year increase until an academy shall be formed whereby this place to great splendour will have attained, for which, next to God, the Honorable Company which shall have sent such teacher here shall have laud and praises. For our own part we shall endeavor to find a fit place in which the schoolmaster shall hold his school."

The desired "gerund-grinder" — to use Tristram Shandy's word — was soon despatched. The fit place was found, — a good house with a garden. He was promised an annual salary of five hundred guilders. Each scholar also was to pay six guilders per quarter. But Dr. Curtius's lines fell in difficult places; he could keep no order among his Latin-school pupils, those bad young New Amsterdamites, who "beat each other and tore the clothes from each other's backs," and he complained he was restrained by the orders of parents from properly punishing them. (I may say here that I have not found that

COLONIAL DAYS

New York schoolmasters were ever as cruel as were those of New England.) A graver matter to honest colonists was his charging a whole beaver-skin too much per quarter to some scholars, and soon he was packed back to Holland. His successor, a young man of twenty-two, who had been tutor to Stuyvesant's sons, had better luck, better control, and a better academy; and New Amsterdam to "great splendour was attained," having pupils from other towns and colonies, even from so far away as Virginia.

The relations between church, school, and state were equally close throughout all New Netherland. Thus, in 1661, Governor Stuyvesant recommended Charles De Bevoise as schoolmaster for Brooklyn; and when Domine Henricus Selyns left the Brooklyn church, Schoolmaster De Bevoise was ordered to read prayers and sermons, "to read a postille" every Sabbath until another minister was obtained. He was also a *krankebesoecker*, or comforter of the sick. Even after the establishment of English rule in the colony, the connection of Dutch church and school was equally close. When Johannis Van Eckellen was engaged by the Consistory of the Dutch church in Flatbush in October, 1682, as a schoolmaster for the town, it was under this extremely interesting and minute contract, which, translated, reads thus: —

ARTICLES OF AGREEMENT made with Johannis Van Eckellen, schoolmaster and clerk of the church at Flatbush.

1st. The school shall begin at eight o'clock in the morning, and go out at eleven o'clock. It shall begin again at one o'clock and end at four o'clock. The bell shall be rung before the school begins.

2nd. When the school opens, one of the children shall read the morning prayer, as it stands in the catechism, and close with the prayer before dinner. In the afternoon it shall begin with the prayer after dinner, and close with the evening prayer. The evening school shall begin with the Lord's Prayer, and close by singing a Psalm.

3rd. He shall instruct the children in the common prayers and the questions and answers of the catechism, on Wednesdays and Saturdays, to enable them to say their catechism on Sunday afternoons in the church before the afternoon service, otherwise on the Monday following, at which the schoolmaster shall be present. He shall demean himself patient and friendly towards the children in their instruction, and be active and attentive to their improvement.

COLONIAL DAYS

4th. He shall be bound to keep his school nine months in succession, from September to June, one year with another, or the like period of time for a year, according to the agreement with his predecessor, he shall, however, keep the school nine months, and always be present himself.

CHURCH SERVICE.

ART. 1st. He shall be chorister of the church, ring the bell three times before service, and read a chapter of the Bible in the church, between the second and third ringing of the bell; after the third ringing he shall read the ten commandments and the twelve articles of Faith, and then set the Psalm. In the afternoon, after the third ringing of the bell, he shall read a short chapter, or one of the Psalms of David, as the congregation are assembling. Afterwards he shall again set the Psalm.

ART. 2nd. When the minister shall preach at Brooklyn or New Utrecht, he shall be bound to read twice before the congregation a sermon from the book used for the purpose. The afternoon sermon will be on the catechism of Dr. Vander Hagen, and thus he shall follow the turns of the minister. He shall hear the children recite the questions and answers of the catechism, on that Sunday, and he shall instruct them. When the minister preaches at Flatlands, he shall perform the like service.

ART. 3rd. He shall provide a basin of water for the baptisms, for which he shall receive twelve stuyvers, in wampum, for every baptism, from the parents or sponsors. He shall furnish bread and wine for the communion, at the charge of the church. He shall furnish the minister, in writing, the names and ages of the children to be baptized, together with the names of the parents and sponsors; he shall also serve as a messenger for the consistories.

ART. 4th. He shall give the funeral invitations, and toll the bells, for which service he shall receive, for persons of fifteen years of age and upwards, twelve guilders; and for persons under fifteen, eight guilders. If he shall invite out of the town, he shall receive three additional guilders for every town; and if he shall cross the river to New York, he shall have four guilders more.

SCHOOL MONEY.

He shall receive for a speller or reader in the day school three guilders for a quarter, and for a writer four guilders.

In the evening school, he shall receive for a speller or reader four guilders for a quarter, and for a writer five guilders.

SALARY.

The remainder of his salary shall be four hundred guilders in wheat, of wampum value, deliver-

COLONIAL DAYS

able at Brooklyn Ferry; and for his service from October to May, two hundred and thirty-four guilders in wheat, at the same place, with the dwelling, pasturage, and meadow appertaining to the school to begin the first day of October.

I agree to the above articles, and promise to observe the same to the best of my ability.

JOHANNIS VAN ECKELLEN.

Truly we have through this contract — to any one with any powers of historic imagination — a complete picture of the duties of the schoolmaster of that day.

When the English came in power in 1664, some changes were made in matters of education in New York, but few changes in any of the conditions in Albany. Governor Nicholls, on his first visit up the river, made one significant appointment, — that of an English schoolmaster. This was the Englishman's license to teach: —

"Whereas the teaching of the English Tongue is necessary in this Government; I have, therefore, thought fitt to give License to John Shutte to bee the English Schoolmaster at Albany: and upon condition that the said John Shutte shall not demand any more wages from each Scholar than is given by the Dutch to their Dutch Schoolmasters. I have further granted to the said John Shutte that hee shall bee the only English Schoolmaster at Albany."

The last clause of this license seems superfluous; for it is very doubtful whether there was for many years any other English teacher who eagerly sought what was so far from being either an onerous or lucrative position. Many generations of Albany children grew to manhood ere the Dutch schoolmasters found their positions supererogatory.

Women-teachers and girl-scholars were of small account in New York in early days. Girls did, however, attend the public schools. We find Matthew Hillyer, in 1676, setting forth in New York that he "hath kept school for children of both sexes for two years past to satisfaction." Dame-schools existed, especially on Long Island, where English influences and Connecticut emigration obtained. In Flushing Elizabeth Cowperthwait was reckoned with in 1681 for "schooling and diet for children;" and in 1683 she received for thirty weeks' schooling, of "Martha Johanna," a scarlet petticoat, — truly a typical Dutch payment. A school bill settled by John Bowne in Flushing in 1695 shows that sixpence a week was paid to the teacher for each scholar who learned reading, while writing and ciphering cost one shilling twopence a week. This, considering the usual wages and prices of the times, was fair pay enough.

We have access to a detailed school bill of the Lloyd boys in 1693, but they were sent away from their Long Island home at Lloyd's Neck to New England; so the information is of no value as a record of a New York school; but one or two of these items are curious enough to be recounted:—

	£	s.	d.
1 Quarter's board for boys	9	7	6
Pd knitting stockings for Joseph		1	4
Pd knitting 1 stocking for Henry			6
Joseph's Schooling, 7 mos.		7	
A bottle of wine for His Mistris			10
To shoo nails & cutting their har			7
Stockins & mittins		3	9
Pd a woman tailor mending their cloaths		3	3
Wormwood & rubab for them			6
To Joseph's Mistris for yearly feast and wine		1	8
Pair gloves for boys		2	6
Drest deerskin for the boys' breeches		1	6

Wormwood and rhubarb for the boys and a feast and wine for the schoolmistress, albeit the wine was but tenpence a bottle, seems somewhat unfair discrimination.

IN OLD NEW YORK

There is an excellent list of the clothing of a New York schoolboy of eleven years given in a letter written by Fitz-John Winthrop to Robert Livingstone in 1690. This young lad, John Livingstone, had also been in school in New England. The "account of linen & clothes" shows him to have been very well dressed. It reads thus:—

Eleven new shirts
4 p^r laced sleves
8 plane cravets
4 cravets with lace
4 stripte wastecoats with black buttons
1 flowered wastecoat
4 new osinbrig britches
1 gray hat with a black ribbon
1 gray hat with a blew ribbon
1 dousin black buttons
1 dousin coloured buttons

3 pr gold buttons
3 pr silver buttons
2 p^r fine blew stockings
1 pr fine red stockins
4 white handkerchiefs
2 speckled handkerchiefs
3 pair gloves
1 stuff coat with black buttons
1 cloth coat
1 pr blew plush britches
1 pr serge britches
2 combs
1 pr new shoees

Silk & thred to mend his clothes.

In 1685 Goody Davis taught a dame-school at Jamaica; and in 1687 Rachel Spencer died in Hempstead, and her name was recorded as that of a schoolmistress. In 1716, at the Court of Sessions in Westchester, one of the farm-wives, Dame Shaw, complained that "a travelling woman who came out of ye Jerseys who kept school at several places in Rye parish, hath left with her a child eleven months old, for which she desires relief from the parish."

It is easy to fancy a vague romance through this short record of the life of this nameless "travelling woman" who, babe in arms, earned a scanty living by teaching, and who at last abandoned the school and the child whose birth may, perhaps, have sent her a nameless wanderer in a strange country, — for "the Jerseys" were far away from Rye parish in those days.

There was a schoolmistress in Hempstead at a later date. She was old in 1774. I don't know her name, but I know of the end of her days. The vestry allowed her forty shillings, "to be dealt out to her a little at a time, *so as to last her all winter.*" She lived through that luxurious winter, and died in 1775. Her coffin cost twelve shillings, and Widow Thurston was paid six shillings for digging the grave for her old crony and gossip. Schoolmistresses were not many on Long Island, — can we wonder at it? Had this dame been one of the penniless church-poor in a Dutch community (which Hempstead was not), she would probably have had forty shillings a month instead of a winter, and a funeral that would have been not only decent in all the necessities of a funeral, but a triumph of prodigality in all the comforts and pleasures of the mortuary accompaniments of the day, such as wine, rum, beer, cakes, tobacco, and pipes.

The "book-learning" afforded to colonial girls in New York was certainly very meagre. Mrs. Anne Grant wrote of the first quarter of the eighteenth century:—

"It was at that time very difficult to procure the means of instruction in those island districts; female education was, of consequence, conducted on a very limited scale; girls learned needlework (in which they were indeed both skilful and ingenious) from their mothers and aunts; they were taught, too, at that period to read, in Dutch, the Bible, and a few Calvinistic tracts of the devotional kind. But in the infancy of the settlement few girls read English; when they did, they were thought accomplished; they generally spoke it, however imperfectly, and few were taught writing."

William Smith, the historian of New York, writing during the year 1756 of his fellow townswomen, and of education in general in New York, gives what was doubtless a true picture of the inelegance of education in New York: —

"There is nothing they [New York women] so generally neglect as Reading, and indeed all the Arts for the improvement of the Mind, in which I confess we have set them the Example. Our Schools are in the Lowest Order, the Instructors want Instruction, and through a long, shameful neglect of the Arts and Sciences our Common Speech is very corrupt, and the Evidences of a Bad Taste both as to thought and Language are visible in all our Proceedings publick and private."

One obstacle to the establishment and success of schools and education was the hybridization of language. New Yorkers spoke neither perfect Dutch nor good English. It was difficult in some townships to gather an English-speaking jury; hence, naturally, neither tongue could be taught save in the early and simpler stages of education. It was difficult for those little Dutchmen who heard Holland-Dutch spoken constantly at home to abandon it entirely and speak English in the schools. The Flatbush master (himself a Dutchman, but bound to teach English) invented an ingenious plan to crowd out the use of Dutch in school. He carried a little metal token which he gave each day to the first scholar whom he heard use a Dutch word. That scholar could promptly turn the token over to any other scholar whom he likewise detected in using Dutch, and he in turn could do the same. Thus the token passed from hand to hand through the day; but the unlucky wight who chanced to have possession of it when the school day was over was soundly whipped.

In default of "spilling," as one master wrote in his receipts, and in which he was somewhat shaky himself, he and all other colonial teachers took a firm stand on "cyphering." "The Bible and figgers is all I want my boys to know," said one old farmer. When the school session opened and closed, as we have seen in Flatbush, with prayer and praise, with catechism every day, and special catechising twice a week, even "figgers" did not have much of a chance. All the old Dutch primers that I have seen, the *Groot A B C boeks zeer bekwaam voor de yongekinderen te leeren*, contain nothing (besides the alphabet) but religious sentences, prayers, verses of the Bible, pious rhymes, etc.; and dingy little books they are, not even up to the standard of our well-known New England Primer.

Though the Dutch were great printers of horn-books, I do not find that they were universal users of those quaint little "engines of learning." If used in Dutch-American schools, none now survive the lapse of two centuries; and indeed only one can be found in a Holland museum. Mr. Tuer, the historian of the horn-book, states that there is one in the museum at Antwerp, printed by H. Walpot, of Dordrecht, Netherlands, in 1640; and a beautiful silver-backed Dutch horn-book in the collection of an English clergyman at Coombe Place, England; and a few others in public libraries that are probably Dutch. Dutch artists show, by their frequent representations of horn-books in paintings of children, that the little *a-b-boordje* was well known. In the "Christ blessing Little Children," by Rembrandt, the presentment of a child has a horn-book hanging at his side. In several pictures by Jan Steen, 1626–79, horn-books may be noted; in one a child has hung his horn-book on a parrot's perch while he plays. In 1753 English children used horn-books in New York as in the other provinces, for they were advertised with Bibles and primers in the New York newspapers at that time.

Printed arithmetics were rarely used or seen. Schoolmasters carried with them carefully executed "sum-books" in manuscript, from which scholars copied the sums and rules into small blank-books of their own. One, of a Gravesend scholar in 1754, has evidently served to prove the pupil's skill both in arithmetic and penmanship. The book is prefaced by instructive aphorisms, such as "Carefully mind to mend in every line;" "Game not in school when you should write." The wording of the rules is somewhat curious. One reads: —

"Rule of Bartar, which is for exchanging of ware, One Commodity for another. This Rule shows the Merchants how they may Proportion their Goods so that neither of them may sustain loss. Sum. Two Merchants A. and B. bartar. A. hath 320 Dozen of Candles @ 4/6 per Dozen; for which B. giveth him £30 in Cash and ye Rest in Cotton @ 8d per lb. I demand: how much Cotton B. must give A. more than the £30 in Cash."

COLONIAL DAYS

As commerce increased and many young men sought a seafaring life, navigation was taught, and advanced mathematics. In 1749 the notice of a Brooklyn "Philomath" on Nassau Island shows that he could teach "Arithmetick vulgar and decimal; Geometry plain and Spherical; Surveying, Navigation in 3 kinds, viz: Plain Mercator and Great Circle Sailing, Astronomy, and Dialling." Thus did this Philomath meet the demand of the day. In 1773 the Flatbush Grammar School was taught by John Copp, who also took scholar-boarders, who "have the advantage of being taught geography in the winter evenings, with many other useful particulars that frequently occur to the teacher," which seems to present a rather melancholy picture when we reflect on the other particulars of good coasting and skating that then were around Flatbush, on the *Steenbakkery* for instance, which, doubtless, would frequently occur on winter evenings to the scholar-boarder.

IN OLD NEW YORK

CHAPTER III

WOOING AND WEDDING

THE domestic life of the Dutch settlers flowed on in a smooth-running and rather dull stream, varying little through either honor-bearing or discreditable incident from day to day. Any turbulence of dissension or divorce between husband and wife was apparently little known and certainly little noted. Occasionally an entry which tells of temporary division or infelicity can be unearthed from the dingy pages of some old court-record, thereby disclosing a scene and actors so remote, so shadowy, so dimmed with the dust of centuries, that the incident often bears no semblance of having happened to real living folk, but seems rather to pertain to a group of inanimate puppets. One of these featureless, colorless, stiff Dutch marionettes is Anneke, the daughter of boisterous old Domine Schaets, the first minister at Fort Orange.

A fleeting glimpse of her marital infelicity is disclosed through the record of her presence in Albany under the shadow of some unexplained and now forgotten scandal. To satisfy her father's virtuous and severe congregation, she refrained from contaminating attendance at Communion. The domine resented this condition of affairs, and refused to appear before the Consistory though summoned four times by the *bode*. He persisted in irritatingly " ripping up new differences and offences; " and he disregarded with equal scorn the summons of a magistrate to appear before the Court; and he was therefore suspended from his clerical office. All was at last " arranged in love and friendship," leaving out the dispute about " Universal Grace," which I suppose could not be settled ; but daughter Anneke was ordered off to New York to her husband, " with a letter of recommendation; and as she was so headstrong, and would not depart without the Sheriff's and Constable's interference, her disobedience was annexed to the letter." It is pleasing to know, from the record of an " Extraordinary Court holden in Albany" a month later, — in July, 1681, — of a very satisfactory result in the affairs of the young couple.

"Tho: Davidtse promisses to conduct himself well and honorably towards his wife Anneke Schaets, to Love and never neglect her, but faithfully and properly to maintain and support her with her children according to his means, hereby making null and void all questions that have occurred and transpired between them both, never to repeat them, but are entirely reconciled: and for better assurance of his real Intention and good Resolution to observe the same, he requests that two good men be named to oversee his conduct at New York towards his said wife, being entirely disposed and inclined to live honorably and well with her as a Christian man ought, subjecting himself willingly to the rule and censure of the said men. On the other hand his wife Anneke Schaets, promisses also to conduct herself quietly and well and to accompany him to New York with her children and property, not to leave him any more, but to serve and help him and with him to share the sweets and the sours as becomes a Christian spouse: Requesting all differences which had ever existed between them both may be hereby quashed and brought no more to light or cast up, as she on her side is heartily disposed to. Their Worship of the Court Recommend parties on both Sides to observe strictly their Reconciliation now made, and the gentleman at New York will be informed that the matter is so far arranged."

COLONIAL DAYS

We can certainly add the profound hope, after all this quarrelling and making up, after all those good promises, that Anneke's home was no longer " unregulated and poorly kept," as was told of her by the Labadist travellers during their visit to Albany at that time. The appointing of " two good men " as arbitrators or overseers of conduct was very usual in such cases; thereby public adjustment in open court of such quarrels was avoided.

Tender parents could not unduly shelter a daughter who had left her husband's bed and board. He could promptly apply to the court for an order for her return to him, and an injunction to her parents against harboring her. It has been plain to see in all such cases which I have chanced upon in colonial records that the Court had a strong leaning towards the husband's side of the case; perhaps thinking, like Anneke Schaets, that the wife should "share the sweets and the sours like a Christian spouse."

In 1697 Daniel Vanolinda petitioned that his wife be " ordyred to go and live with him where he thinks convenient." The wife's father was promptly notified by the Albany magistrates that he was " discharged to shelter her in his house or elsewhere, upon Penalty as he will answer at his Perill;" and she returned to her husband.

In the year 1665 a New Amsterdammer named Lantsman and his wife, Beletje, were sorely estranged, and went to the courts for settlement of these differences. The Court gave the matter into the hands of two of the Dutch ministers, who were often assigned the place of peacemakers. As usual, they ordered the parents of Beletje to cease from harboring or abetting her. The husband promised to treat her well, but she answered that he always broke his promises to her. He was determined and assiduous to retrieve her, and finally was successful; thus they were not made " an example to other evil housekeepers." A curious feature of this marriage quarrel is the fact that this Lantsman, who was so determined to retain his wife, had been more than recreant about marrying her. The banns had been published, the wedding-day set, but Bridegroom Lantsman did not appear. Upon being hauled up and reprimanded, his only proffered excuse was the very simple one that his clothes were not ready.

COLONIAL DAYS

When Anniatje Fabritius requested an order of court for her husband to vacate her house with a view of final separation from him, it was decided by the arbitrators that no legal steps should be taken, but that "the parties comport themselves as they ought, in order that they win back each other's affections, leaving each other in meanwhile unmolested"—which was very sensible advice. Another married pair having "met with great discouragement" (which is certainly a most polite expression to employ on such a subject), agreed each to go his and her way, after an exact halving of all their possessions.

Nicasius de Sille, magistrate of New Utrecht and poet of New Netherland, separated his life from that of his wife because—so he said—she spent too much money. It is very hard for me to think of a Dutch woman as "expensefull," to use Pepys' word. He also said she was too fond of schnapps,—which her respected later life did not confirm. Perhaps he spoke with poetic extravagance, or the nervous irritability and exaggeration of genius. Albert Andriese and his wife were divorced in Albany in 1670, " because strife and difference hath arisen between them." Daniel Denton was divorced from his wife in Jamaica, and she was permitted to marry again, by the new provincial law of divorce of 1672. These few examples break the felicitous calm of colonial matrimony, and have a few companions during the years 1670–72; but Chancellor Kent says "for more than one hundred years preceding the Revolution no divorce took place in the colony of New York;" and there was no way of dissolving a marriage save by special act of Legislature.

Occasionally breach-of-promise suits were brought. In 1654 Greetje Waemans produced a marriage ring and two letters, promissory of marriage, and requested that on that evidence Daniel de Silla be "condemned to legally marry her." He vainly pleaded his unfortunate habit of some days drinking too much, and that on those days he did much which he regretted; among other things, his bacchanalian love-making of Greetje. François Soleil, the New Amsterdam gunsmith, another recreant lover, swore he would rather go away and live with the Indians (a terrible threat) than marry the fair Rose whom he had left to droop neglected — and unmarried.

COLONIAL DAYS

One curious law-case is shown by the injunction to Pieter Kock and Anna van Voorst. They had entered into an agreement of marriage, and then had been unwilling to be wedded. The burgomasters and *schepens* decided that the promise should remain in force, and that neither should marry any other person without the permission of the other and the Court; but Anna did marry very calmly (when she got ready) another more desirable and desired man without asking any one's permission.

It certainly gives us a great sense of the simplicity of living in those days to read the account of the suit of the patroon of Staten Island in 1642 against the parents of a fair young Elsje for loss of services through her marriage. She had been bound out to him as a servant, and had married secretly before her time of service had expired. The bride told the worshipful magistrates that she did not know the young man when her mother and another fetched him to see her; that she refused his suit several times, but finally married him willingly enough, — in fact, eloped with him in a sail-boat. She demurely offered to return to the Court, as compensation and mollification, the pocket-handkerchief which was her husband's wedding-gift to her. Two years later, Elsje (already a widow) appeared as plaintiff in a breach-of-promise suit; and offered, as proof of her troth-plight, a shilling-piece which was her second lover's not more magnificent gift. Though not so stated in the chronicle, this handkerchief was doubtless given in a "marriage-knot,"— a handkerchief in which was tied a gift of money. If the girl to whom it was given untied the knot, it was a sign of consent to be speedily married. This fashion of marriage-knots still exists in parts of Holland. Sometimes the knot bears a motto; one reads when translated, "Being in love does no harm if love finds its recompense in love; but if love has ceased, all labor is in vain. Praise God."

Though second and third marriages were common enough among the early settlers of New Netherland, I find that usually attempts at restraint of the wife were made through wills ordering sequent loss of property if she married again. Nearly all the wills are more favorable to the children than to the wife. Old Cornelius Van Catts, of Bushwick, who died in 1726, devised his estate to his wife Annetje with this gruff condition: "If she happen to marry again, then I geff her nothing of my estate, real or personal. But my wife can be master of all by bringing up to good learning my two children. But if she comes to marry again, then her husband can take her away from the farm." John Burroughs, of Newtown, Long Island, in his will dated 1678 expressed the general feeling of husbands towards their prospective widows when he said, "If my wife marry again, then her husband must provide for her as I have."

Often joint-wills were made by husband and wife, each with equal rights if survivor. This was peculiarly a Dutch fashion. In Fordham in 1670 and 1673, Claude de Maistre and his wife Hester du Bois, Pierre Cresson and his wife Rachel Cloos, Gabriel Carboosie and Brieta Wolferts, all made joint-wills. The last-named husband in his half of the will enjoined loss of property if Brieta married again. Perhaps he thought there had been enough marrying and giving in marriage already in that family, for Brieta had had three husbands, — a Dane, a Frieslander, and a German, — and his first wife had

had four, and he — well, several, I guess; and there were a number of children; and you could n't expect any poor Dutchman to find it easy to make a will in all that confusion. In Albany may be found several joint-wills, among them two dated 1663 and 1676; others in the Schuyler family. There is something very touching in the thought of those simple-minded husbands and wives, in mutual confidence and affection, going, as we find, before the notary together and signing their will together, "out of love and special nuptial affection, not thereto misled or sinisterly persuaded," she bequeathing her dower or her father's legacy or perhaps her own little earnings, and he his hard-won guilders. It was an act significant and emblematic of the ideal unison of interests and purposes which existed as a rule in the married life of these New York colonists.

Mrs. Grant adds abundant testimony to the domestic happiness and the marital affection of residents of Albany a century later. She states: —

"Inconstancy or even indifference among married couples was unheard of, even where there happened to be a considerable disparity in point of intellect. The extreme affection they bore their mutual offspring was a bond that forever endeared them to each other. Marriage in this colony was always early, very often happy, and very seldom indeed interested. When a man had no son, there was nothing to be expected with a daughter but a well brought-up female slave, and the furniture of the best bed-chamber. At the death of her father she obtained another division of his effects, such as he thought she needed or deserved, for there was no rule in these cases.

"Such was the manner in which those colonists began life; nor must it be thought that those were mean or uninformed persons. Patriots, magistrates, generals, those who were afterwards wealthy, powerful, and distinguished, all, except a few elder brothers, occupied by their possessions at home, set out in the same manner; and in after life, even in the most prosperous circumstances, they delighted to recount the 'humble toils and destiny obscure' of their early years."

Weddings usually took place at the house of the bride's parents. There are some records of marriages in church in Albany in the seventeenth century, one being celebrated on Sunday. But certainly throughout the eighteenth century few marriages were within the church doors. Mrs. Vanderbilt says no Flatbush marriages took place in the church till within the past thirty or forty years. In some towns written permission of the parents of the groom, as well as the bride, was required by the domine before he would perform the marriage ceremony. In the Guelderland the express consent of father and mother must be obtained before the marriage; and doubtless that custom of the Fatherland caused its adoption here in some localities. The minister also in some cases gave a certificate of permission for marriage; here is one given by "ye minister at Flatbush," —

Isaac Hasselburg and Elizabeth Baylis have had their proclamation in our church as commonly our manner and custom is, and no opposition or hindrance came against them, so as that they may be confirmed in ye banns of Matrimony, whereto we wish them blessing. Midwout ye March 17th, 1689.

RUDOLPH VARRICK, *Minister.*

This was probably to permit and authorize the marriage in another parish.

Marriage fees were not very high in colonial days, nor were they apparently always retained by the minister; for in one of Domine Selyns's accounts of the year 1662, we find

COLONIAL DAYS

him paying over to the Consistory the sum of seventy-eight guilders and ten stuyvers for fourteen marriage fees received by him. The expenses of being married were soon increased by the issuing of marriage licenses. During the century dating from the domination of the British to the Revolutionary War nearly all the marriages of genteel folk were performed by special permission, by Governor's license, the payment for which (a half-guinea each, so Kalm said) proved through the large numbers a very welcome addition to the magistrates' incomes. It was in fact deemed most plebeian, almost vulgar, to be married by publication of the banns for three Sundays in church, or posting them according to the law, as was the universal and fashionable custom in New England. This notice from a New York newspaper, dated December 13, 1765, will show how widespread had been the aversion to the publication of banns: —

"We are creditly informed that there was married last Sunday evening, by the Rev. Mr. Auchmuty, a very respectable couple that had published three different times in Trinity Church. A laudable example and worthy to be followed. If this decent and for many reasons proper method of publication was once generally to take place, we should have no more of clandestine marriages; and save the expense of licenses, no inconsiderable sum these hard and depressing times."

Another reason for "crying the banns" was given in Holt's "New York Gazette and Postboy" for December 6, 1765.

"As no Licenses for Marriage could be obtained since the first of November for Want of Stamped Paper, we can assure the Publick several Genteel Couple were publish'd in the different Churches of this City last Week; and we hear that the young Ladies of this Place are determined to Join Hands with none but such as will to the utmost endeavour to abolish the Custom of marrying with License which Amounts to many Hundred per annum which might be saved."

Severe penalties were imposed upon clergymen who violated the law requiring license or publication ere marriage. The Lutheran minister performed such a marriage, and the *schout's* "conclusion" as to the matter was that the offending minister be flogged and banished. But as he was old, and of former good services, he was at last only suspended a year from power of preaching.

COLONIAL DAYS

Rev. Mr. Miller, an English clergyman writing in 1695, complains that many marriages were by justices of the peace. This was made lawful by the States-General of Holland from the year 1590, and thus was a law in New Netherland. By the Duke's Laws, 1664, it was also made legal. This has never been altered, and is to-day the law of the State.

Of highly colored romance in the life of the Dutch colonists there was little. Sometimes a lover was seized by the Indians, and his fair betrothed mourned him through a long life. In one case she died after a few years of grief and waiting, and on the very day of his return from his savage prison to his old Long Island home he met the sad little funeral procession bearing her to the grave. Another humbler romance of Gravesend was when a sorrowing widower fell in love with a modest milkmaid at first sight as she milked her father's cows; ere the milking was finished he told his love, rode to town on a fast horse for a governor's license, and married and carried off his fair Grietje. A century later a fair Quakeress of Flushing won in like manner, when milking, the attention and affection of Walter Franklin of New York.

Another and more strange meeting of lovers was when young Livingstone, the first of the name in New York, poor and unknown, came to the bedside of a dying Van Rensselaer in Albany to draw up a will. The dying man, with a jealousy stronger than death, said to his beautiful wife, Alida Schuyler, "Send him away, he will be your second husband;" and he was,—perhaps the thought provoked the deed.

Even if there were few startling or picturesque romances or brilliant matches, there was plenty of ever-pleasant wooing. New Amsterdam was celebrated, just before its cession to the English, for its young and marriageable folk and its betrothals. This is easily explained; nearly all the first emigrants were young married people, and the years assigned to one generation had passed, and their children had grown up and come to mating-time. Shrewd travellers, who knew where to get good capable wives, wooed and won their brides among the Dutch-American fair ones. Mr. Valentine says: "Several of the daughters of wealthy burghers were mated to young Englishmen whose first occasions were of a temporary character." The beautiful surroundings of the little town tempted all to love-making, and the unchaperoned simplicity of society aided early " matching." The Locust-Trees, a charming grove on a bluff elevation on the North River a little south of the present Trinity Churchyard, was a famous courting-place; or tender lovers could stroll down the " Maiden's Path; " or, for still longer walks, to the beautiful and baleful " Kolck," or " Collect," or " Fresh Water," as it was sequentially called; and I cannot imagine any young and susceptible hearts ever passing without some access of sentiment through any green field so sweetly named as the " Clover Waytie."

There were some curious marriage customs, — some Dutch, some English. One very pretty piece of folk-lore, of bride-honoring, was brought to my notice through the records of a lawsuit in the infant town of New Harlem in 1663, as well as an amusing local pendant to the celebration of the custom. It seems that a certain young Harlem couple were honored in the pleasant fashion of the Fatherland, by having a " May-tree " set up in front of their dwelling-place. But certain gay young sparks of the neighborhood, to anger the groom and cast ridicule on his marriage, came with unseemly noise of blowing of horns, and hung the lovely May-tree during the night with ragged stockings. We never shall know precisely what special taunt or insult was offered or signified by this over-ripe crop of worn-out hosiery; but it evidently answered its tantalizing purpose, for on the morrow, at break of day, the bridegroom properly resented the "mockery and insult," cut down the hateful tree, and committed other acts of great wrath; which, being returned in kind (for thrice was the stocking-full tree set up), developed a small riot, and thus the whole affair was recorded. Among the State Papers at Albany are several letters relating to another insulting "stocking-tree" set up in Albany at about the same date, and also fiercely resented.

Collections for the church poor were sometimes taken at weddings, as was the universal custom for centuries in Holland. When Stephanus Van Cortlandt and Gertrude Schuyler were married in Albany, in 1671, thirteen guilders six stuyvers were contributed at the wedding, and fifteen guilders at the reception the following day. At the

COLONIAL DAYS

wedding of Martin Kreiger, the same year, eleven guilders were collected; at another wedding the same amount. When the daughter of Domine Bogardus was married, it was deemed a very favorable time and opportunity to take up a subscription for building the first stone church in New Amsterdam. When the wedding-guests were all mellow with wedding-cheer, " after the fourth or fifth round of drinking," says the chronicle, and, hence generous, each vied with the other in good-humored and pious liberality, they subscribed " richly." A few days later, so the chronicle records, some wished to reconsider the expensive and expansive transaction at the wedding-feast, and " well repented it." But Director Kieft stiffly held them to their contracts, and " nothing availed to excuse."

It is said that the English drink of posset was served at weddings. From the " New York Gazette " of February 13, 1744, I copy this receipt for its manufacture: —

" A Receipt for all young Ladies that are going to be Married. To Make a

SACK-POSSET.

From famed Barbadoes on the Western Main
Fetch sugar half a pound; fetch sack from Spain

A pint; and from the Eastern Indian Coast
Nutmeg, the glory of our Northern toast.
O'er flaming coals together let them heat
Till the all-conquering sack dissolves the sweet.
O'er such another fire set eggs, twice ten,
New born from crowing cock and speckled hen;
Stir them with steady hand, and conscience pricking
To see the untimely fate of twenty chicken.
From shining shelf take down your brazen skillet,
A quart of milk from gentle cow will fill it.
When boiled and cooked, put milk and sack to egg,
Unite them firmly like the triple League.
Then covered close, together let them dwell
Till Miss twice sings: *You must not kiss and tell.*
Each lad and lass snatch up their murdering spoon,
And fall on fiercely like a starved dragoon."

Many frankly simple customs prevailed. I do not know at how early a date the fashion obtained of "coming out bride" on Sunday; that is, the public appearance of bride and groom, and sometimes entire bridal party in wedding-array, at church the Sunday after the marriage. It certainly was a common custom long before Revolutionary times, in New England as well as New York; but it always seems to me more an English than a Dutch fashion. Mr. Gabriel Furman, in his manuscript Commonplace Book, dated 1810, now owned by the Long Island Historical Society, tells of one groom whom he remembered who appeared on the first Sunday after his marriage attired in white broadcloth; on the second, in brilliant blue and gold; on the third, in peach-bloom with pearl buttons. The bride's dress, wholly shadowed by all this magnificence, is not even named. Mrs. Vanderbilt tells of a Flatbush bride of the last century, who was married in a fawn-colored silk over a light-blue damask petticoat. The wedding-waistcoat of the groom was made of the same light-blue damask, — a delicate and deferential compliment. Often it was the custom for the bridal pair to enter the church after the service began, thus giving an opportunity for the congregation to enjoy thoroughly the wedding-finery. Whether bride and groom were permitted to sit together within the church, I do not know. Of course ordinarily the seats of husband and wife were separate. It would seem but a poor show, with the bride in a corner with a lot of old ladies, and the groom up in the gallery.

On Long Island the gayety at the home of the bride's parents was often followed on the succeeding day by "open house" at the house of the groom's parents, when the wedding-party, bridesmaids and all, helped to keep up the life of the wedding-day. An old letter says of weddings in the city of New York: —

"The Gentlemen's Parents keep Open house just in the same manner as the Bride's Parents. The Gentlemen go from the Bridegroom's house to drink Punch with and give Joy to his Father. The Bride's visitors go in the same manner from the Bride's to her mother's to pay their compliments to her. There is so much driving about at these times that in our narrow streets there is some danger. The Wedding-house resembles a bee-hive. Company perpetually flying in and out."

All this was in vogue by the middle of the last century. There was no leaving home by bride and groom just when every one wanted them,— no tiresome, tedious wedding-journey; all cheerfully enjoyed the presence of the bride, and partook of the gayety the wedding brought. In the country, up the Hudson and on Long Island, it was lengthened out by a bride-visiting, — an entertaining of the bridal party from day to day by various hospitable friends and relations for many miles around; and this bride-visiting was usually made on horseback.

COLONIAL DAYS

Let us picture a bride-visiting in springtime on Long Island, where, as Hendrick Hudson said, "the land was pleasant with grass and flowers and goodly trees as ever seen, and very sweet smells came therefrom." The fair bride, with her happy husband; the gayly dressed bridesmaids, in silken petticoats, and high-heeled scarlet shoes, with rolled and powdered hair dressed with feathers and gauze, riding a-pillion behind the groom's young friends, in satin knee-breeches, and gay coats and cocked hats, — all the accompanying young folk in the picturesque and gallant dress of the times, and gay with laughter and happy voices, — a sight pretty to see in the village streets, or, fairer still, in the country lanes, where the woods were purely starred and gleaming with the radiant dogwood; or roads where fence-lines were " white with blossoming cherry-trees as if touched with lightest snow; " or where pink apple-blossoms flushed the fields and dooryards; or, sweeter far, where the flickering shadows fell through a bridal arch of the pale green feathery foliage of the abundant flowering locust-trees, whose beautiful hanging racemes of exquisite pink-flushed blossoms cast abroad a sensuous perfume like orange blossoms, which fitted the warmth, the glowing sunlight, the fair bride, the beginning of a new life; — let us picture in our minds this June bride-visiting; we have not its like to-day in quaintness, simplicity, and beauty.

CHAPTER IV

TOWN LIFE

THE earlier towns in New Netherland gathered usually closely around a fort, both for protection and companionship. In New Amsterdam, as in Albany, this fort was an intended refuge against possible Indian attacks, and also in New Amsterdam the established quarters in the new world of the Dutch West India Company. As the settlement increased, roads were laid out in the little settlement leading from the fort to any other desired point on the lower part of the island. Thus Heere Straat, the Breede Weg, or Broadway, led from the fort of New Amsterdam to the common pasture-lands. Hoogh Straat, now Stone Street, was evolved from part of the road which led down to the much-used Ferry to Long Island, at what is now Peck Slip. Whitehall Street was the shortest way to the East River. In front of the fort was the Bowling Green. Other streets were laid out, or rather grew, as needs increased. They were irregular in width and wandering in direction. They were not paved nor kept in good order, and at night were scarcely lighted.

In December, 1697, city lamps were ordered in New York "in the dark time of the moon, for the ease of the inhabitants." Every seventh house was to cause a lanthorn and candle to be hung out on a pole, the expense to be equally shared by the seven neighbors, and a penalty of ninepence was decreed for every default. And perhaps the watch called out in New York, as did the watch in Old York, in London and other English cities, "Lanthorne, and a whole candell-light! Hang out your lights here." An old chap-book has a watchman's rhyme beginning, —

"A light here! maids, hang out your light,
And see your horns be clear and bright
That so your candle clear may shine," etc.

Broad Street was in early days a canal or inlet of the sea, and was called De Heere Graft, and extended from the East River to Wall Street. Its waters, as far as Exchange

Place, rose and fell with the tide. It was crossed by several foot-bridges and a broader bridge at Hoogh Straat, or Stone Street, which bridge became a general meeting-place, a centre of trade. And when the burghers and merchants decided to meet regularly at this bridge every Friday morning, they thus and then and there established the first Exchange in New York City. It is pleasant to note, in spite of the many miles of city growth, how closely the exchange centres have remained near their first home. In 1660 the walks on the banks of the Graft were paved, and soon it was bordered by the dwellings of good citizens; much favored on account of the homelikeness, so Mr. Janvier suggests, of having a good, strong-smelling canal constantly under one's nose, and ever-present the pleasant familiar sight of squat sailor-men and squat craft before one's eyes. In 1676, when simple and primitive ways of trade were vanishing and the watercourse was no longer useful or needful, the Heere Graft was filled in — reluctantly, we can believe — and became Broad Street.

The first mention of street-cleaning was in 1695, when Mr. Vanderspiegle undertook the job for thirty pounds a year. By 1701 considerable pains was taken to clean the city, and to remove obstructions in the public ways. Every Friday dirt was swept by each citizen in a heap in front of his or her house, and afterwards carted away by public cartmen, who had threepence a load if the citizen shovelled the dirt into the cart, sixpence if the cartman loaded his cart himself. Broad Street was cleaned by a public scavenger at a salary of $40 per annum paid by the city; for the dirt from other streets was constantly washed into it by rains, and it was felt that Broad Street residents should not be held responsible for other people's dirt. Dumping-places were established. Regard was paid from an early date to preserving "the Commons." It was ordered that lime should not be burnt thereon; that no hoopsticks or saplings growing thereon should be cut; no timber taken to make into charcoal; no turfs or sods carried away therefrom; no holes dug therein; no rubbish be deposited thereon.

Within the city walls all was orderly and quiet. "All persons who enter yͤ gates of yͤ citty with slees, carts and horses, horseback, not to ride faster than foot-tap." The carters were forced to dismount and walk at their horses' heads. All moved slowly in the town streets. Living in a fortified town, they still were not annoyed by discharge of guns, for the idle "fyring of pistells and gunns" was prohibited on account of "ill-conveniants."

The first houses were framed and clap-boarded; the roofs were thatched with reeds; the chimneys were catted, made of logs of wood filled and covered with clay; sometimes even of reeds and mortar, — for there were, of course, at first no bricks. Hayricks stood in the public streets. Hence fires were frequent in the town, breaking out in the wooden catted chimneys; and the destruction of the inflammable chimneys was decreed by the magistrates. In 1648 it was ordered in New Amsterdam that no "wooden or platted chimney" should be built south of the Freshwater Pond. Fire-wardens — *brandt-meesters* — were appointed, who searched constantly and pryingly for "foul chimney-harts," and fined careless housekeepers therefor when they found them.

It is really surprising as well as amusing to see how the citizens resented this effort for their safety, this espionage over their hearthstones; and especially the wives resented the snooping in their kitchens. They abused the poor *schout* who inspected the chimney-hearths, calling him "a little cock, booted and spurred," and other demeaning names. In 1658 Maddaleen Dirck, as she passed the door of the fire-warden, called out tantalizingly to him, "There is the chimney-sweep at his door,— his chimney is always well-swept." She must have been well scared and truly repentant at the enormity of her offence when she was brought up before the magistrates and accused of having "insulted the worshipful fire-warden on the highway, and incited a riot."

In spite of vigilance and in spite of laws, foul chimneys were constantly found. We hear of the town authorities "reciting that they have long since condemned flag-roofs, and wooden and platted chimneys, but their orders have been neglected, and several fires have occurred; therefore they amplify their former orders as follows: All flag-roofs, wooden chimneys, hay-barracks, and haystacks shall be taken down within four months, in the penalty of twenty-five guilders."

COLONIAL DAYS

The magistrates further equipped the town against conflagration by demanding payment of a beaver skin from each house, to purchase with the collected sum two hundred and fifty leather fire-buckets from the Fatherland. But delays were frequent in ocean transportation, and the shoemakers in town finally made the fire-buckets. They were placed in ten groups in various houses throughout the town. For their good order and renewal, each chimney was thereafter taxed a guilder a year. By 1738, two engines with small, solid wooden wheels or rollers were imported from England, and cared for with much pride.

In Albany similar wooden chimneys at first were built; we find contractors delivering reeds for roofs and chimneys. "Fire-leathes" and buckets were ordered. Buckets were owned by individuals and the town; were marked with initials for identification. Many stood a century of use, and still exist as cherished relics. The manner of bucket-service was this: As soon as an alarm of fire was given by shouts or bell-ringing, all citizens of all classes at once ran to the scene of the conflagration. All who owned buckets carried them, and from open windows other fire-buckets were flung out on the streets by persons who were delayed for a few moments by any cause. The running crowd seized the buckets, and on reaching the fire a double line was made from the fire to the river. The buckets filled with water were passed up the line to the fire, the empty buckets down. Any one who attempted to break the line was promptly soused with a bucket of water. When all was over, the fire-warden took charge of the buckets, and as soon as possible the owners appeared, and each claimed and carried home his own buckets.

There was a police department in New Amsterdam as well as a fire department. In 1658 the burgomasters and *schepens* appointed a *ratel-wacht*, or rattle-watch, of ten watchmen, of whom Lodewyck Pos was Captain. Their wages were high, — twenty-four stuyvers (about fifty cents) each a night, and plenty of firewood. The Captain collected fifty stuyvers a month from each house, — not as has since been collected in like manner for the private bribing of the police, but as a legalized method of paying expenses. The rules for the watch are amusing, but cannot be given in full. They sometimes slept on

COLONIAL DAYS

duty, as they do now, and paid a fine of ten stuyvers for each offence. They could not swear, nor fight, nor be "unreasonable;" and "when they receive their quarter-money, they shall not hold any gathering for drink nor any club meeting."

Attention is called to one rule then in force: "If a watchman receive any sum of money as a fee, he shall give the same to the Captain; and this fee so brought in shall be paid to the City Treasurer" — oh the good old times!

The presence of a considerable force of troops was a feature of life in some towns. The soldiers were well cared for when quartered within the fort, sleeping on good, soft, goose-feather beds, with warm homespun blankets and even with linen sheets, all hired from the Dutch *vrouws;* and supplied during the winter with plentiful loads of firewood, several hundred, through levy on the inhabitants; good hard wood, too, — "no watte Pyn wood, willige, oly noote, nor Lindewood" (which was intended for English, but needs translation into "white pine, willow, butternut, nor linden").

No doubt the soldiers came to be felt a

great burden, for often they were billeted in private houses. We find one citizen writing seriously what reads amusingly like modern slang,— that "they made him weary." Another would furnish bedding, provisions, anything, if he need not have any soldier-boarders assigned to him. One of the twenty-three clauses of the "Articles of Surrender" of the Dutch was that the "townsmen of Manhattans shall not have any soldiers quartered upon them without being satisfied and paid for them by their officers." In Governor Nicholl's written instructions to the commander at Fort Albany, he urges him not to lend "too easey an eare" to the soldiers' complaints against their landlords.

Since in the year 1658 the soldiers of New Amsterdam paid but twenty cents a week for quarters when lodged with a citizen, it is not surprising that their presence was not desired. A soldier's pay was four dollars a month.

They were lawless fellows, too lazy to chop wood for their fires; they had to be punished for burning up for firewood the stockades they were enlisted to protect. Their duties were slight, — a drill in the morning, no sentry work during the day, a watch over the city gates at night, and cutting wood. The military code of the day reveals a very lax condition of discipline; it wasn't really much of an army in Dutch days. And as for the Fort and the Battery in the town of New Amsterdam, read Mr. Janvier's papers thereon to learn fully their innocuous pretence of warlikeness.

There was very irregular foreign and inland mail service. It is with a retrospectively pitying shiver that we read a notice, as late as 1730, that "whoever inclines to perform the foot-post to Albany this winter may make application to the Post-Master." Later we find the postmaster leisurely collecting the mail during several weeks for "the first post to Albany this winter." Of course this foot-post was only made when the river was frozen over; swift sloops carried the summer mail up the river in two or three weeks, — sometimes in only ten days from New York to Albany. I can fancy the lonesome post journeying alone up the solemn river, under the awe-full shadow of old Cro'nest, sometimes climbing the icy Indian paths with *ys-sporen*, oftener, I hope, skating swiftly along, as a good son of a Hollander should, and longing every inch of the way for spring and the "breaking-up" of the river.

In 1672, "Indian posts" carried the Albany winter mail; trustworthy redmen, whose endurance and honesty were at the service of their white friends.

The first regular mail started by mounted post from New York for Boston on January 1, 1673. His "portmantles" were crammed with letters and "small portable goods" and "divers bags." He was "active, stout, indefatigable, and honest." He could not change horses till he reached Hartford. He was ordered to keep an eye out for the best ways through forests, and accommodations at fords, ferries, etc., and to watch for all fugitive soldiers and servants, and to be kind to all persons journeying in his company. While he was gone eastward a locked box stood in the office of the Colonial Secretary at New York to collect the month's mail. The mail the post brought in return, being prepaid, was carried to the "coffee-house," put on a table, well thumbed over by all who cared to examine it, and gradually

COLONIAL DAYS

distributed, two or three weeks' delay not making much difference any way.

As in all plantations in a new land, there was for a time in New Netherland a lack of servants. Complaints were sent in 1649 to the States-General of "the fewness of boors and farm-servants." Domestic servants were not found in many households; the capable wife and daughters performed the housework and dairy work. As soon as servants were desired they were speedily procured from Africa. The Dutch brought the first negro slaves to America. In the beginning these slaves in New Netherland were the property of the Dutch West India Company, which rented their services. The company owned slaves from the year 1625. when it first established its authority, and promised to each patroon twelve black men and women from ships taken as prizes. In 1644 it manumitted twelve of the negroes who had worked faithfully nearly a score of years in servitude. In 1652 the Government in Holland consented to the exportation of slaves to the colony for sale. In 1664 Governor Stuyvesant writes of an auction of negroes that they brought good prices, and were a great relief to the garrison in supplying funds to purchase food. Thus did the colony taste the ease of ill-gotten wealth. Though the Duke of York and his governors attempted to check the slave-trade, by the end of the century the negroes had increased much in numbers in the colony. In the Kip family were twelve negro house-servants. Rip van Dam had five; Colonel de Peyster and the Widow Van Courtlandt had each seven adult servants. Colonel Bayard, William Beeckman, David Provoost, and Madam Van Schaick each had three.

On Long Island slaves abounded. It is the universal testimony that they were kindly treated by the Dutch, — too kindly, our English lady thought, who rented out her slaves. Masters were under some bonds to the public. They could not, under Dutch rule, whip their slaves without authorization from the government. The letters in the Lloyd Collection in regard to the slave Obium are striking examples of kindly consideration, and of constant care and thought for his comfort and happiness.

The wages of a hired servant-girl in New York in 1655 were three dollars and a half a month, which was very good pay when we consider the purchasing power of money at that time. It is not till the eighteenth century that we read of the beginning of our vast servant-supply of Irish servants.

There was much binding out of children and young folk for terms of service. In Stuyvesant's time several invoices of Dutch children from the almshouses were sent to America to be put to service, and the official letters concerning them show much kindliness of thought and intent towards these little waifs and strays. Early in the next century a sad little band of Palatines was bound out in New York families. It may prove of interest to give one of the bonds of indenture of a house-servant in Albany.

"THIS INDENTURE witnesseth that Aulkey Hubertse, Daughter of John Hubertse, of the Colony of Rensselaerwyck deceased hath bound herself as a Meniall Servant, and by these presents doth voluntary and of her own free will and accord bind herself as a Meniall Servant unto John Delemont of the City of Albany, weaver, by and with the consent of the Deacons of the Reformed Dutch Church in the Citty of Albany, who are as overseers in the disposal of the said Aulkey Hubertse to serve from the date of these present Indentures unto the full end and term of time that the said Aulkey Hubertse shall come to Age, all which time fully to be Compleat and ended, during all which term the said servant her said Master faithfully shall serve, his secrets keep, his lawful commands gladly everywhere obey, she shall do no Damage to her said Master nor see it to be done by others without letting or giving notice thereof to her said Master: she shall not waste her Master's goods or lend them unlawfully to any. At Cards, Dice, or any unlawful Game she shall not play whereby her said Master may have Damage: with her own goods or the goods of others during the said Term, without License from her said Master she shall neither buy or sell: she shall not absent herself day or night from her Master's service without his Leave, nor haunt Ale-houses, Taverns, or Playhouses, but in all things as a faithful servant, she shall behave herself towards her said Master and all his during the said Term. And the said Master during the said Term, shall find and provide sufficient Wholesome and compleat meat and drink, washing, lodging, and apparell and all other Necessarys fit for such a servant: and it is further agreed between the said Master and Servant in case the said Aulkey Hubertse should contract Matrimony before she shall come to Age then the said Servant is to be free from her said Master's service by virtue thereof: and at the expiration of her said servitude, her said Master John Delemont shall find provide for and deliver unto his said servant double apparell, that is to say, apparell fit for to have and to wear as well on the Lords Day as working days, both linning and woolen stockings and shoes and other Necessarys meet for such a servant to have and to wear, and for the true performance of all and every of said Covenant and Agreements the said parties bind themselves unto each other by these presents."

This indenture was signed and sealed in the year 1710, and varied little from those of previous years. Sometimes the apparel was fully described, and was always good and substantial — and Sunday attire was usually furnished. Sarah Davis, bound out in Albany in 1684, was to be taught to read and knit stockings; was to have silk hoods and a silk scarf for church wear, and substantial petticoats and waistcoats, some of homespun, some of "jersey-spun," others of "carsoway," which was kersey.

"Redemptioners," bound for a term of service as domestic and farm servants, also came from the various European States; and good servants often did they prove, and good citizens, too, when their terms of service expired. There also opened in this emigration of redemptioners a vast opportunity for adventure. In the "New York Gazette" of March 15, 1736, we read of one servant-girl adventurer: —

"We hear that about two years ago a certain Irish gentlewoman was brought into this province a servant, but she pretended to be a great fortune worth some thousands (was called the Irish Beauty). Her master confirming the same a certain young man (Mr. S***ds), courted her; and she seemingly shy, her master for a certain sum of money makes up the match, and they were married and go to their country-seat; but she not pleased with that pursuades her husband to remove to the city of New York and set up a great tavern. They did so. Next she pursuades her husband to embark for Ireland to get her great portion. When he comes there he finds her mother a weeder of gardens to get bread. In his absence Madam becomes acquainted with one Davis, and they sell and pack up her husband's effects, which were considerable, and embark for North Carolina. When they come there they pass for man and wife, and he first sells the negroes and other effects, then sells her clothes and at last he sells her for a servant, and with the produce returns to his wife in Rhode Island, he having made a very good voyage."

They were constantly eloping with their masters' or mistresses' wardrobes, sometimes with portions of both, and setting up as gentlefolk on their own account. We find one Jersey girl running a fine rig: dressed in a velvet coat and scarlet knee-breeches, with a sword, cocked hat, periwig, and silken hose, she had a gay carouse in New York tap-houses and tea-gardens, as long as her stolen twenty pounds lasted; but with an empty stomach, she ceased to play the lad, and went sadly to the stone ketch. I turn regretfully from the redemptioners; they were the most picturesque and romance-bearing element of the community.

But little is known of the early practice of medicine in New Netherland, less than of the other American colonies, and that little is not of much importance. It must be remembered that the times were what Lowell has felicitously termed the twilight through which alchemy was passing into chemistry, and the science of medicine partook of mysticism. Astrology and alchemy were not yet things of the past. From the beginning of the settlement the West India Company paid a surgeon (Jacob Varravanger was the name of one) to live in New Amsterdam and care for the health of the Company's "servants." But soon so many "freemen" came — that is, not in the pay of the Company — that some doubts arose in the minds of the Council whether it would not be better to save the salary, by trusting to independent practitioners. There were three such in New Amsterdam in 1652. They made pills and a terrible dose of rhubarb, senna, and port-wine, called "Vienna Drink." But folk were discouragingly healthy in the little town in spite of poor water, and lack of drainage, and filth in the streets, and the Graft. Van der Donck said, "Galens have meagre soup in that country;" and soon the poor doctors, to add to their income, petitioned the Director that none but surgeons should be allowed to shave people. This was a weighty matter, and after profound consideration, the Council gave the following answer: —

"That shaving doth not appertain exclusively to *chirugery*, but is only an appanage thereof. That no man can be prevented from operating herein upon *himself*, or doing another this friendly act, provided that it be through *courtesy*, and that he do not receive any money for it, and do not keep an open-shop of that sort, which is hereby forbidden, declaring in regard to the last request, this act to belong to *chirugery* and the health of man."

COLONIAL DAYS

And the surgeons on shore were protected against the ship barbers, who landed and who made some pretty grave mistakes when attempting to doctor in the town. In 1658 Dr. Varravanger, somewhat disgusted at the treatment of the sick, who, if they had no families, had to trust to the care of strangers, established the first New York Hospital, which was, after all, only a clean and suitable house with fire and wood and one good woman to act as matron.

There was no lack of physicians, — half a dozen by 1650. A century later, the historian of the province pronounced the towns to be swarming with quacks.

One tribute to old-time medicine and New York medical men we owe still. The well-known Kiersted Ointment manufactured and sold in New York to-day is made from a receipt of old Dr. Hans Kiersted's, the best colonial physician of his day, who came to New York in 1638. The manufacture of this ointment is a closely guarded family secret. He married the daughter of the famous Anneke Jans; and, in the centuries that have passed, the descendants have had more profit from the ointment than from the real estate. There were plenty of "wise women" to care for the increase of the populace; the New Amsterdam midwife had a house built for her by the government. It was a much respected calling. The mother of Anneke Jans was a midwife. They were licensed to practise. Here is an appointment by the Governor in 1670: —

"Whereas I am given to understand that Tryntje Meljers ye wife of Wynant Vander pool a sworn and approved midwife at Albany in which Imployment she hath Continued for ye span of fourteen years past in good reputation not refusing her assistance but on ye contrary affording her best help to ye poorer sorte of people out of Christian Charity, as well as to ye richer sorte for reward, and there being severall other less skilfull women who upon occasion will pretend to be midwives where they can gain by it but refuse their helpe to ye poore. These presents Certifye That I doe allow of ye said Tryntje Meljers to be one of ye profest sworne midwives at Albany, and that she and one more skilfull woman be only admitted to Undertake ye same there except upon Extraordinary occasions. They continuing their Charitable assistance to ye poore & a diligent attendance on their calling."

The small number of settlers, the exigencies and hardships of a planter's life, the absence of luxuries, as well as the simplicity of social manners among the Dutch, prohibited anything during the rule of the Dutch in New Netherland which might, by a long and liberal stretch of phraseology or idealization of a revered ancestry, be termed fashionable life.

They occasionally had a merry dinner. Captain Beaulieu, a gay Frenchman who brought a prize into port, gave a costly one for fourteen persons; and as he did not pay for it, it has passed into history. Governor Stuyvesant had a fine dinner given to him on the eve of one of his "gallant departures." De Vries has left us an amusing account of a quarrelsome feast given by the gunner of the Fort. Eating and drinking were ever the Dutchman's pleasures.

With the establishment of English rule there came to the town of the Governor's residence, in the Province of New York as in the other provinces, a little stilted attempt at the semblance of a court.

Formal endeavors to have something of the nature of a club were made under the English governors, to promote a social feeling in the town. A letter of the day says,

IN OLD NEW YORK

"Good correspondence is kept between the English and Dutch; to keep it closer sixteen families (ten Dutch and six English) have had a constant meetting at each other's houses in Turnes twice every week in winter and now in summer once. They meet at six at night, and part at about eight or nine." The exceedingly early hours of these social functions seem to accent the simplicity of the life of the times even more than the absence of any such meetings would have done. The arrival of a new Governor was naturally an important and fashionable event. When the Earl and Countess of Bellomont landed in New York in 1698 they were, of course, greeted first with military salutes; four barrels of gunpowder made sufficient noise of welcome. Then a great dinner to a hundred and fifty people was given. It was presided over by the handsomest man in town, Mayor de Peyster, and the fare consisted of "venison, turkey, chicken, goose, pigeon, duck and other game; mutton, beef, lamb, veal, pork, sausages; with puddings, pastry, cakes and choicest of wines." It was a fine welcome, but such dinners did not come every day to the Governor; he had other and sorrier gatherings in store. Soon we hear of him shut up eight days in succession in Albany (as he said in his exceedingly plain English) "in a close chamber with fifty sachems, who besides the stink of bear's grease with which they were plentifully bedaubed, were continually smoking and drinking of rum," and coming back to town in a "nasty slow little sloop." No wonder he fell dangerously sick with the gout.

Mrs. Grant, writing of New York society in the middle of the eighteenth century, said: —

"At New York there was always a governor, a few troops, and a kind of little court kept; there was a mixed, and in some degree polished society. To this the accession of many families of French Huguenots rather above the middling rank, contributed not a little."

This little important circle had some fine balls. On January 22, 1734, one was given at the Fort on the birthday of the Prince of Wales, which lasted till four in the morning. Another was given in honor of the King's birthday. "The ladies made a splendant appearance. Sometimes as many as a hundred persons were present and took part."

Occasionally a little flash of gossiping brightness shows us a picture of the everyday life of the times in the capital town. Such a bit of eighteenth-century scandal is the amusing account, from Mrs. Janet Montgomery's unpublished Memoirs, of Lady Cornbury, wife of the Governor, Lord Cornbury. She died in New York in 1706, much eulogized, and most ostentatiously mourned for by her husband. Mrs. Montgomery's account of her is this: —

"The lady of this very just nobleman was equally a character. He had fallen in love with her ear, which was very beautiful. The ear ceased to please and he treated her with neglect. Her pin-money was withheld and she had no resource but begging and stealing. She borrowed gowns and coats and never returned them. As hers was the only carriage in the city, the rolling of the wheels was easily distinguished, and then the cry in the house was 'There comes my lady; hide this, hide that, take that away.' Whatever she admired in her visit she was sure to send for next day. She had a fancy to have with her eight or ten young ladies, and make them do her sewing work, for who could refuse their daughters to my lady."

COLONIAL DAYS

What a picture of the times! the fashionable though impecunious Englishwoman and the score of industrious young Dutch-American seamstresses sitting daily and most unwillingly in the Governor's parlor.

One of the most grotesque episodes in New York political history, or indeed in the life of any public official, was the extraordinary notion of this same Governor, Lord Cornbury, to dress in women's clothes. Lord Stanhope and Agnes Strickland both assert that when Cornbury was appointed Governor and told he was to represent her Majesty Queen Anne, he fancied he must dress as a woman. Other authorities attribute his absurd masquerade to his fond belief that in that garb he resembled the Queen, who was his cousin. Mrs. Montgomery said it was in consequence of a vow, and that in a hoop and head-dress and with **fan in hand** he was frequently seen in the evening on the ramparts. A portrait of him owned by Lord Hampton shows him in the woman's dress of the period, fan in hand. Truly it was, as Lewis Morris wrote of him to the Secretary of State, "a peculiar and detestable magot," and one which must have been most odious and trying to honest, manly New Yorkers, and especially demoralizing to the soldiers before whom he paraded in petticoats. When summarily deposed by his cousin from his governorship, he was promptly thrust into a New York debtor's prison, where he languished till the death of his father made him third Earl of Clarendon.

COLONIAL DAYS

CHAPTER V

DUTCH TOWN HOMES

THE first log houses of the settlers, with their "reeden roofs," were soon supplanted by a more substantial form of edifice, Dutch, naturally, in outline. They were set with the gable-end to the street and were often built of Dutch brick, or, at any rate, the gable-ends were of brick.

Madam Knights' description of the city of New York and the houses is wonderfully clear, as is every account from her graphic pen, but very short:—

"The Buildings are Brick Generaly, very stately and high though not altogether like ours in Boston. The Bricks in some of the Houses are of divers Coullers and laid in Checkers, being glazed, look very agreable. The inside of them is neat to admiration; the wooden work, for only the walls are plaster'd, and the Sumers and Gist are planed and kept very white scour'd as so is all the partitions if made of Bords."

IN OLD NEW YORK

Albany long preserved its Dutch appearance and Dutch houses. Peter Kalm's description of the city of Albany is a good one, and would well answer for other New York towns: —

"The houses in this town are very neat, and partly built with stones covered with shingles of the White Pine. Some are slated with tiles from Holland, because the clay of this neighborhood is not reckoned fit for tiles. Most of the houses are built in the old way, with the gable-end towards the street; the gable-end of brick and all the other walls of planks. The gutters on the roofs reach almost to the middle of the street. This preserves the walls from being damaged by the rain, but it is extremely disagreeable in rainy weather for the people in the streets, there being hardly any means of avoiding the water from the gutters.

"The street doors are generally in the middle of the houses and on both sides are seats, on which, during fair weather the people spend almost the whole day, especially on those which are in the shadow of the houses. In the evening these seats are covered with people of both sexes, but this is rather troublesome, as those who pass by are obliged to greet everybody unless they will shock the politeness of the inhabitants of this town. The streets are broad and some of them are paved; in some parts they are lined with trees. The long streets are almost parallel to the river, and the others intersect them at right angles."

COLONIAL DAYS

Rev. Samuel Chandler, chaplain of one of the Massachusetts regiments, stopped several days in Albany in the year 1755. He tells of the streets with rows of small button-trees, of the brick houses curiously flowered with black brick and dated with the same, the Governor's house having "two black brick-hearts." The houses one story high with their gable-ends "notched like steps" (he might have said with corbel-steps), were surmounted with vanes, the figures of horses, lions, geese, and sloops. There were window shutters with loop-holes outside the cellars. Smith, the historian of New York, writing at the same time, calls the houses of all the towns, "built of brick in Dutch taste." Daniel Denton, writing as early as 1670, tells of the "red and black tile (of New York) giving at a distance a pleasing aspect to the Spectators." All the old sketches of the town which exist, crude as they are, certainly do present a pleasing aspect.

The chief peculiarity of these houses were the high roofs; some were extraordinarily steep and thus afforded a garret, a loft, and a cock-loft. There was reason and economy in this form of roof. The shingle covering was less costly than the walls, and the contraction in size of second-story rooms was not great.

Very few of the steep roofs in the earliest days had eave-troughs, hence the occasional use in early deeds and conveyances of the descriptive term "free-drip." At a later date troughs were made of sections of the bark of some tree (said to be birch) which the Indians brought into town and sold to house builders. Then came metal spouts projecting several feet, as noted by Kalm. In 1789, when Morse's Geography was issued, he speaks of the still projecting water-spouts or gutters of Albany, "rendering it almost dangerous to walk the streets on a rainy day;" but in New York more modified fashions obtained long before that time.

The windows were small; some had two panes. When we learn that the ordinary panes of glass imported at that time were in size only six inches by eight inches, we can see that the windows were only loopholes.

The front doors were usually divided as in Holland, into an upper and lower half. They were in early days hung on strap-hinges, afterwards on heavy iron hinges. In the upper half of the door, or in a sort of transom over the door, were set two round bull's-eyes of heavy greenish glass, just as are seen in Holland. Often the door held a knocker of brass or of iron. The door usually opened with a latch.

The inventories of the household effects of many of the early citizens of New York might be given, to show the furnishings of these homes. I choose the belongings of Captain Kidd to show that "as he sailed, as he sailed" he left a very comfortable home behind him. He was, when he set up housekeeping with his wife Sarah in 1692, not at all a bad fellow, and certainly lived well. He possessed these handsome and abundant house furnishings:—

One dozen Turkey work chairs.
One dozen double-nailed leather chairs.
Two dozen single-nailed leather chairs.
One Turkey worked carpet.
One oval table.
Three chests of drawers.
Four looking-glasses.
Four feather beds, bolsters, and pillows.
Three suits of curtains and valances.
Four bedsteads.
Ten blankets.
One glass case.
One dozen drinking-glasses.
Four tables.
Five carpets or rugs.
One screen frame.
Two stands.
One desk.

Two dressing boxes.
One close stool.
One warming pan.
Two bed pans.
Three pewter tankards.
Four kettles.
Two iron pots.
One skillet.
Three pairs of fire irons.
One pair of andirons.
Three chafing dishes.
One gridiron.
One flesh fork.
One brass skimmer.
Four brass candlesticks.
Two pewter candlesticks.
Four tin candlesticks.
One brass pestle.
One iron mortar.
2½ dozen pewter plates.
Five pewter basins.
Thirteen pewter dishes.
Five leather buckets.
One pipe Madeira wine.
One half-pipe " "
Three barrels pricked cider.
Two pewter salt-cellars.
Three boxes smoothing irons.
Six heaters.
One pair small andirons.
Three pairs tongs.
Two fire shovels.
Two fenders.
One spit.
One jack.
One clock.
One coat of arms.
Three quilts.

Parcel linen sheets, table cloths, napkins, value thirty dollars.

One hundred and four ounces silver plate, value three hundred dollars.

The early New Englanders sat in their homes on stools and forms, and very rarely on chairs. It is not so easy to know of Dutch furnishings, for the words *stoel* and *setel* and *banck*, which are found in early inventories, all mean a chair, but also may not have meant in colonial days what we now designate as a chair. A *stoel* was really a seat of any kind; and *stoels* there were in plenty among the first settlers. As Cowper says:

COLONIAL DAYS

" Necessity invented stools,
Convenience next suggested elbow-chairs,
And Luxury the accomplished Sofa last."

In this natural succession came the seats of the colonists. The leather chairs with double rows of nails — in Captain Kidd's list — were a very substantial and handsome piece of furniture.

Tables there were in all houses, and looking-glasses in all well-to-do homes. The stands of Captain Kidd were small tables. The carpets named after the tables were doubtless table-covers. The early use of the word was always a cover for a table.

A truly elegant piece of furniture — one in use by well-to-do folk in all the colonies — was a cupboard. Originally simply a table for the display of cups and other vessels, it came to have shelves and approach in form our sideboard. An inventory of a New York citizen of the year 1690 names a " Holland cupboard furnished with earthenware and purslin" worth fifteen pounds. Another owned a French nut-wood cupboard of about the same value. Cupboard-cloths usually accompanied them. A few of these cupboards still exist, usually their exact history forgotten, but still known as "Holland cupboards." As long as the inventories of estates of deceased persons were made out and registered with much minuteness of detail, a single piece of furniture could be traced readily from heir to heir, but unfortunately only the older inventories display this minuteness.

One unusual word may be noted, which is found in New York inventories, *boilsted*, *bilsted*, or *billsted* — as "a boilsted bed," "a boilsted bureau." The "Century Dictionary" gives *bilsted* as the native name of the American sweet-gum tree, the liquidambar, but Mr. Watson says *boilsted* or *bilsted* meant maple, — hence these articles meant a bureau of maplewood, etc.

A very common form of bedstead in early days, both in town and farm houses, was the one built into the house, scarcely more than a bench to hold the bedding, usually set into an alcove or recess. In a contract for the "Ferry House," built in Brooklyn in 1665 (the house in which the ferry-master lived), we read one clause thus: "to wainscot the east side the whole length of the house, and in the recess two bedsteads (betste) one in the front room and one in the inside room, with a pantry at the end of the bedstead."

This alcove *betste* was much like a cupboard; it had doors which closed over it when unoccupied and shut it from view. This does not seem very tidy from our modern point of view, but the heavily curtained and upholstered beds of other countries gave but little more opportunity of airing. Adam Roelandsen, the first New York schoolmaster, had these *betste* built in his house; and Jan Peeck, the founder of Peekskill, had four *betste* in his country home, as certainly were needed by a man who had — so he said — "a house full of children and more besides."

The *sloep-banck*, or *slaw-bunk*, was another form, a folding-bed. This was also set within closet doors or hanging curtains. It was an oblong frame filled in with a network of rope or strips of wood, set apart like the slats of a bed. This frame was fastened to the wall at one end, the bed's head, with heavy hinges; and at night it was placed in a horizontal position, and the unhinged end, or foot of the bed, was supported on heavy turned legs which fitted into sockets in the frame. When not in use, the frame was hooked up against the wall and covered with the curtains or doors.

Other *sloep-bancks* were stationary. One sold in Albany in 1667 to William Brouwer was worth ten guilders. Parson Chandler as late as 1755 said the beds in Albany were simply wooden boxes, each with feather-bed, undersheet, and blanket cover. The kermis bed, on which the Labadist fathers slept in Brooklyn, was a pallet bed. Another bedstead often named was the *trecke-bedde*, or the *sloep-banck ap rollen*, which, as its name implies, was on rollers. It was a trundle-bed, and in the daytime was rolled under a high-post bedstead, if there were one in the room, and concealed by the valance of calico or chiney.

The beds were deep and soft, of prime geese feathers. For many years the custom obtained of sleeping on one feather-bed and under another of somewhat lighter weight. The pillow-cases, called "pillow-bears," or pillow-clothes, were often of checked linen. The hangings of the bed when it was curtained were also, in families of moderate means, of checked and striped linen, in wealthier houses of kidderminster, camlet, and harrateen. With English modes of living came English furniture; among other innovations the great carved four-poster, which, richly hung with valances and tester, was, as Mrs. Grant said, "the state-bed, the family Teraphim, secretly worshipped and only exhibited on rare occasions." The bedsteads of Captain Kidd with valances and curtains were doubtless four-posters.

A notable feature in the house-furnishing of early colonial days was the abundance and good quality of household linen. The infrequency of regular washing seasons and times (often domestic washing took place but once in three or four months) made a large amount of bed, table, and personal linen a matter of necessity in all thrifty, tidy households. One family, in 1704 (not a very wealthy one), had linen to the amount of five hundred dollars. Francis Rombout, one of the early mayors of New York, had, at the time of his death, in the year 1690, fifty-six diaper napkins, forty-two coarse napkins and towels, thirteen table-cloths of linen and diaper, fifty-one "pillow-bears," thirty sheets, four bolster-covers, ten checked "pillow-bears," two calico cupboard-cloths, six table-cloths, four check chimney-cloths, two of linen; worth in all, twenty-one pounds eleven shillings.

Mynheer Marius, who was worth about fifteen thousand dollars, — a rich man, — had eight muslin sheets, twenty-three linen sheets, thirty-two pillow-cases, two linen table-cloths, seven diaper table-cloths, sixty-one diaper napkins, three "ozenbergs" napkins, sixteen small linen cupboard-cloths. Colonel William Smith of Long Island was not so rich as the last-named Dutch merchant, but he had six hundred dollars' worth of linen. John Bowne, the old Quaker of Flushing, Long Island, recorded in his diary, in 1691, an account of his household linen. He had four table-cloths, a dozen napkins, a dozen towels, six fine sheets, two cotton sheets, four coarse linen sheets, two fine tow sheets, two bolster cases, nine fine pillow-biers, four coarse pillow-biers.

In 1776, the house furnishings of a house in Westchester County in the "Neutral Ground," were removed on account of the war. The linen consisted of fifty-one linen sheets, eleven damask table-cloths, one linen table-cloth, twenty-one homespun cloths, four breakfast cloths, twelve damask napkins, fifty-six homespun napkins, fifteen towels, twenty-nine pillow-cases.

This linen was usually kept in a great linen chest often brought from Holland. Made of panelled oak or of cedar, these chests were not only useful, but ornamental. They were substantial enough to have lasted till our own day, unless wantonly destroyed as clumsy and cumbersome, and a few have survived.

There was one display of wealth which was not wholly for the purpose of exhibiting the luxury and refinement of the housekeeper, but also served as a safe investment of surplus funds, — household silver. From early days silver tankards, spoons, dram-cups, and porringers appear in inventories. Salt-cellars and beakers are somewhat rare; but as years crept on, candlesticks, salvers, coffee-pots, teakettles, snuffers, bread-baskets, and punch-bowls are on the list. When Captain Kidd, the pirate, was a happy bridegroom in 1692, as a citizen of respectability and social standing, he started housekeeping with three hundred dollars' worth of silver. Magistrate Marius had at the same time a silver tankard, three salt-cellars, two beakers, a mustard pot and spoon, twenty-seven sweetmeat spoons, four tumblers, nine cups each with two ears, a salver, a mug and cover, a baby's chafing-dish, a fork and cup. Governor Rip van Dam had in silver three tankards, a chafing-dish, three castors, two candlesticks, snuffers and tray, two salvers, a mug, salt-cellar and pepper-pot, and a large number of spoons. Abraham de Peyster had a splendid array: four tankards, two decanters, two dishes, three plates, eleven salvers, two cups and covers, two chafing-dishes, six porringers, four sauce-boats, two punch-bowls, three mugs, four sugar-dishes, a coffee-pot and tea-pot, seven salts and shovels, a saucepan, four pairs snuffers and stand, a mustard-pot, a bread-basket, a dram-bottle, tobacco-dish, nine castors, six candlesticks, one waiter, twenty-three forks, three soup-spoons, two punch ladles, ten table-spoons, ten teaspoons, two sugar-tongs; truly a display fit for a fine English hall. We may note in this, as in many other inventories, that the number of small pieces seems very small and inadequate; ten teaspoons and twenty-three forks appear vastly disproportioned to the great pieces of plate.

These outfits of silver were, of course, unusual, but nearly all families had some pieces; and even on farms there would be seen fine pieces of silver.

Curious forms of Dutch silver were the "bite and stir" sugar boxes, often shell-shaped, with a partition in the middle. On one side was placed the loaf sugar, which could be nibbled with the tea; on the other, the powdered or granulated sugar, which could be stirred into the teacup with a teaspoon. Another graceful piece was the *ooma*, or sifter, for the mixed cinnamon and sugar with which many sprinkled their hot waffles. An *ooma* resembled a muffineer. The name was derived from the Dutch *oom*, an uncle, and the article was a favorite gift of an uncle on the wedding day of niece or nephew. We find Dutch dames leaving by will "milk-pots shaped like a cow," a familiar form of Dutch silver, and can readily believe that much silver owned in New York was made in Holland.

Coming from a country where the manufacture of porcelain and stone-ware was already of much importance, and the importation of Oriental china was considerable, it is not strange that we find more frequent mention of articles of china than in the English colonies. For instance, Mayor Francis Rombouts came to this country as clerk for a Dutch commercial house and died in 1690. He had a cupboard furnished with earthenware and "purslin:" twenty-six earthen dishes, earthen pots, twelve earthen "cupps," six "purslin cupps," six earthen "juggs," six pitchers, which was really a very pretty showing. Doubtless the "purslin" was Delft. In the list of early sales at Fort Orange, earthen-ware appears. In New England, in similar sales, its name would never be seen.

Trim and orderly pieces of furniture, as well as pretty ones, were the various hanging wall-racks for plates, knives, and spoons. I presume they were shaped like the ones still in use in Holland. We find in inventories *lepel-borties* (which were spoon-racks) as early as 1664. When an oaken plate-rack was filled with shining pewter plates, Delft dishes, or even red earthen "Portugese ware," it made a thoroughly artistic decoration for the walls of the old Dutch kitchen. There were also stands or boxes with divisions for holding knives and forks.

CHAPTER VI

DUTCH FARMHOUSES

THE old Dutch homestead of colonial times fitted the place and the race for which it was built. There was plenty of solid level earth for it to stand on, — so it spread out, sunny and long. The men who built it had never climbed hills or lived on mountain-tops, nor did they mean to climb many stairs in their houses. The ceilings were low, the stairs short and steep, and the stories few; a story and a half were enough for nearly every one. The heavy roof, curving slightly inward, often stretched out in front at the eaves to form a shelter for the front stoop. Sometimes in the rear it ran out and down over a lean-to to within six or eight feet from the ground. Sometimes dormer windows broke the long roof-slope and gave light to the bedrooms or garret within. This long roof contracted the walls of the second-story bedrooms, but it afforded a generous, useful garret, which to the Dutch housekeeper was one of the best rooms in the house.

The long side of the house was usually set to receive the southern sunshine; if convenient, the gable-end was turned to the street or lane; for, being built when there were poor roads and comparatively little travel, and when the settlers were few in number, each house was not isolated in lonesome woods or in the middle of each farm, but was set cosily and neighborly just as close to those of the other settlers as the extent of each farm would allow, and thus formed a little village street.

The windows of these houses were small and had solid wooden shutters, heavily hinged with black-painted iron hinges. Sometimes a small crescent-shaped opening cut in the upper portion of the shutter let in a little dancing ray of light at early dawn into the darkened room. In the village as in the city the stoop was an important feature of the house and of home life. Through the summer months the family gathered on this outdoor sitting-room at the close of day. The neighbors talked politics as they smoked their evening pipes, and the young folk did some mild visiting and courting. As the evening and pipes waned, little negro slaves brought comfortiers, or open metal dishes of living coals, to start the smouldering tobacco afresh in the long Dutch pipes.

The cellar of these old farmhouses was a carefully built apartment, for it played a most important part in the orderly round, in the machinery of household affairs. It was built with thought, for it had to be cool in summer and warm in winter. To accomplish the latter result, its few small windows and gratings were carefully closed and packed with salt hay in the autumn, and a single trap-door opening outside the house furnished winter entrance. Within this darkened cellar were vast food-stores which put to shame our modern petty purchases of weekly supplies. There were always found great bins of apples, potatoes, turnips, and parsnips. These vegetables always rotted a little toward spring and sprouted, and though carefully sorted out and picked over sent up to the *kamer* above a semi-musty, damp-earthy, rotten-appley, mouldy-potatoey smell which, all who have encountered will agree, is unique and indescribable. Strongly bound barrels of vinegar and cider and often of rum lay in firm racks in this cellar; and sometimes they leaked a little at the spigot, and added their sharply alcoholic fumes to the other cellar-smells. Great hogsheads of corned beef, barrels of salt pork, hams seething in brine ere being smoked, tonnekens of salted shad and mackerel, firkins of butter, kilderkins of home-made lard, jars of pickles, kegs of pigs' feet, or souse, tumblers of spiced fruits, graced this noble cellar. On a swing-shelf were *rolliches* and head-cheese and festoons of sausages. On such a solid foundation, over such a storage-room of plenty, thrift, and prudence, stood that sturdy edifice, — the home-comfort of the New York farmer.

On the ground-floor above were low-studded rooms, one called the *kamer*, which was the parlor and spare bedroom as well; for on its clean sanded floor often stood the best bedstead, of handsome carved mahogany posts, with splendid high-piled feather-beds, heavy hangings, and homespun linen sheets and pillow-cases. Back of this *kamer*, in the linter, was the milk-room. The spinning-room with its spinning-wheels was the sitting-room, or occasionally the kitchen, and the bedroom adjoining was called the spinning-room *kametje*. There were often four or five spinning-wheels in a family, and their merry hum meant lively work. The furniture of these rooms was in character much like that of townhouses, and all had sanded floors. Above these rooms were comfortable chambers; and above the chambers the garret.

A more loving pen than mine has drawn the old garrets of the Flatbush farmhouses, with their cast-off furniture, old trunks, and bandboxes; the unused cradle and crib; the little end window with its spider-webs and yellow wasps buzzing angrily, and beating with extended wings against the dingy panes, or sitting in dull clusters, motionless and silent, along the moulding; the rough chimneys; the spinning-wheels and looms, the wooden pegs with discarded clothing. Mrs. Vanderbilt says: —

"The shingled roof which overarched the garret in all its length and breadth was discolored by time, and streaked and stained with the leakage caused by hard northeast storms; there were tin-pans and sea-shells apparently placed at random over the floor in a purposeless way, but which were intended to catch the drip when the warped shingles admitted the rain. In winter there were little drifts of snow here and there which had sifted through the nail-holes and cracks."

The garret was a famous drying-place in winter-time for the vast washings. Often long adjustable poles were fitted from rafter to rafter to hold the hanging garments.

In the garret, beside the chimney and opening into it, was the smokehouse, sometimes shaped like a cask. Too heavy and big to have been brought in and up to the garret, it was probably built in it. Around this smokehouse were hung hams and sausages, and sides of bacon and dried beef. These usually were not cured in this garret smokehouse; that was simply a storage-place, in which they could be kept properly dry and a little smoked.

Of the *kamer*, or parlor, of New Amsterdam Irving wrote, with but slight exaggeration of its sanctity and cherished condition: —

"The grand parlor was the *sanctum sanctorum*, where the passion for cleaning was indulged without control. In this sacred apartment no one was permitted to enter excepting the mistress and her confidential maid, who visited it once a week, for the purpose of giving it a thorough cleaning — always taking the precaution of leaving their shoes at the door, and entering devoutly on their stocking-feet. After scrubbing the floor, sprinkling it with fine white sand, which was curiously stroked into angles, and curves, and rhomboids, with a broom — after washing the windows, rubbing and polishing the furniture, and putting a new bunch of evergreens in the fireplace — the window shutters were again closed to keep out the flies, and the room carefully locked up till the revolution of time brought round the weekly cleaning-day."

Mrs. Grant fully confirms and emphasizes this account as applicable to the parlors of country-houses as well.

The kitchen was usually in a long rambling ell at one gable-end of the house, rarely in an ell at right angles to the main house; in it centred the picturesqueness of the farm-house. It was a delightful apartment, bustling with activity, cheerful of aspect. On one side always stood a dresser.

> " Every room was bright
> With glimpses of reflected light
> From plates that on the dresser shone."

The shining pewter plates, polished like silver, were part of every thrifty housewife's store; a garnish of pewter, which was a set of different-sized plates, was often her wedding-gift. Their use lingered till this century, and many pieces now are cherished heirlooms.

Methods of cooking and cooking utensils varied much from those of the present day. The great brick oven was built beside the fireplace; sometimes it projected beyond the exterior of the building. It had a smoke-uptake in the upper part, from which a flue connected with the fireplace chimney. It was heated by being filled with burning dry-wood called oven-wood. When the wood was entirely consumed, the ashes were swept out with an oven-broom called a *boender*. A Dutch oven, or Dutch kitchen, was an entirely different affair. This was made of metal, usually tin, cylindrical in form, and open on one side, which was placed next the fire. Through this ran a spit by which meat could be turned when roasting. A bake-kettle, or bake-pan, was a metal pan which stood up on stumpy legs and was fitted with a tightly fitting, slightly convex cover on which hot coals were placed. Within this bake-pan hot biscuit or a single loaf of bread or cake could be baked to perfection.

Across the chimney was a back-bar, sometimes of green wood, preferably of iron; on it hung pot-hooks and trammels, which under the various titles of pot-hangers, pot-claws, pot-clips, pot-brakes, and crooks, appear in every home-inventory. On those pot-hooks of various lengths, pots and kettles could be hung at varying heights above the fire. Often a large plate of iron, called the fireplate, or fire-back, was set at the back-base of the kitchen chimney, where raged so constant and so fierce a fire that brick and mortar crumbled before it. These fire-backs were often cast in a handsome design, sometimes a Scriptural subject. These chimneys were vast in size; Kalm said you could drive a horse and cart through them. Irving says they were "of patriarchal magnitude, where the whole family enjoyed a community of privileges and had each a right to a corner." Often they were built without jambs. Madam Knights wrote in 1704 of New York townhouses: —

"The fireplaces have no jambs (as ours have), but the backs run flush with the walls, and the hearth is of tiles and is as far out into the room at the ends as before the fire, which is generally five foot in the lower rooms, and the piece over where the mantle-tree should be is made as ours with joiners' work and as I suppose is fastened to iron rods inside."

The kitchen fireplace was high as well as wide, and disclosed a vast smoky throat. When the week's cooking was ended and the Sabbath was approaching, this great fireplace was dressed up, put on its best clothes for Sunday, as did all the rest of the family; across the top was hung a short petticoat, or valance, or little curtain gathered full on a string. This was called a *schouwe-kleedt*, a *schoorsteen valletje*, or sometimes a *dobbelsteetiens valletje*, this latter in allusion to the stuff of which the valance was usually made, — a strong close homespun linen checked off with blue or red. This clean, sweet linen frill was placed, freshly washed and ironed, every Saturday afternoon on the faithful, work-worn chimney while it took its Sunday rest. In some houses there hung throughout the week a *schoorsteen valletje;* in others it was only Sunday gear. This was a fashion from early colonial days for both town and country. In the house of Mayor Rombouts in 1690 were fine chimney-cloths trimmed with fringe and lace, and worth half a pound each, and humbler checked chimney-cloths. Cornelius Steenwyck a few years earlier had in his "great chamber" a still gayer *valletje* of flowered tabby to match the tabby window-curtains. Peter Marius had calico valances for his chimneys.

A description given by a Scotchwoman of fireplaces in Holland at about this date shows very plainly from whence this form of hearth-dressing and chimney were derived: —

"The chimney-places are very droll-like; they have no jams nor lintell, as we have, but a flat grate, and there projects over it a lum in a form of the cat-and-clay lum, and commonly a muslin or ruffled pawn around it."

When tiles were used for facing the fire-place and even for hearths, as they often were in the *kamer*, or parlor, they were usually of Delft manufacture, printed in dull blue with coarsely executed outline drawings of Scriptural scenes. In the Van Cortlandt manor-house, the tiles were pure white. I have some of the tiles taken from the old

Schermerhorn house in Brooklyn, built in the middle of the seventeenth century and demolished in 1895. There were nearly two hundred in each fireplace in the house. The scenes were from the Old Testament, and several, if I interpret their significance aright, from the Apocrypha. The figures are discreetly attired in Dutch costumes. Irving says of these Scripture-tiles: " Tobit and his dog figured to great advantage; Haman swung conspicuously on his gibbet; Jonah appeared most manfully bursting out of the whale, like Harlequin through a barrel of fire." To these let me add the very amusing one of Lazarus leaving his tomb, triumphantly waving the flag of the Netherlands.

Sometimes the space between the open fireplace and the ceiling of the *kamer* was panelled, and it had a narrow ledge of a mantelpiece upon which usually were placed a pair of silver, brass, or pewter candlesticks and a snuffers with tray. Occasionally a *blekker*, or hanging candlestick, hung over the mantel. In some handsome houses the surbase was of tiles and also the staircase; but such luxuries were unusual.

Domestic comfort and kindly charity sat

enthroned in every room of these Dutch homes. Daniel Denton wrote of them as early as 1670: —

"Though their low-roofed houses may seem to shut their doors against pride and luxury, yet how do they stand wide open to let charity in and out, either to assist each other, or relieve a stranger."

In these neighborly homes thrift and simple plenty and sober satisfaction in life had full sway; and these true and honorable modes of living lingered long, even to our own day. On the outskirts of a great city, within a few miles of the centre of our greatest city, still stand some of the farmhouses of Flatbush, whose story has been told *con amore* by one to the manner born. These old homesteads form an object-lesson which we may heed with profit to-day, of the dignity, the happiness, the beauty that comes from simplicity in every-day life.

CHAPTER VII

THE DUTCH LARDER

THERE is no doubt that the Dutch colonists were very valiant trenchermen; more avid, perhaps, of quantity and frequency in their food than exacting of variety. Cardinal Bentivoglio (the diplomatist and historian) writing at the time of the first emigration to New Netherland, says that the greatest pleasures of the Hollanders were those of the table. This love of eating made them provident and lavish of food-stores in emigration; and the accounts of scant supplies, poor fare, and dire starvation which are recorded of other colonies, never have been told of the *vol-gevoedt* Dutch. Then, too, they landed on a generous shore, — no rock-bound coast, — Hendrick Hudson said the finest soil for cultivation that he ever set foot on. The welcoming fields richly nourished and multiplied the Hollanders' store of seeds and roots and grafts. The rye quickly grew so tall that a man could bind the ears together above his head. Van der Donck saw a field of barley in New Netherland in which the barley stems were seven feet high. Domine Megapolensis stated that a Rensselaerwyck *schepen* raised fine crops of wheat on the same field eleven years in succession. Two ripe crops of peas or of buckwheat could be raised on the same land in one season. The soil seemed inexhaustible; and fields and woods also offered to the settlers a rich native larder. Among these American food supplies came first and ever the native Indian corn, or "Turkie-wheat." The Dutch (fond of all cereal foods) took to their liking and their kitchens with speed the various forms of corn-food.

Samp and samp porridge were soon their favorite dishes. Samp is Indian corn pounded to a coarsely ground powder in a mortar. Like nearly all the foods made of the various forms of Indian corn, its name is of Indian derivation, and usually its method of preparation and cooking. Roger Williams wrote of it: —

COLONIAL DAYS

"Nawsamp is a kind of meal pottage unparched. From this the English call their samp; which is the Indian corn beaten and boiled."

Samp porridge was a derivative of Indian and Dutch parentage. It was samp cooked in Dutch fashion, like a *hutespot*, or hodgepot, with salt beef or pork and potatoes and other roots, such as carrots and turnips. These were boiled together in a vast kettle, usually in large quantity, as the porridge was better liked after several days' cooking. A week's supply for a family was often cooked at one time. After much boiling a strong crust was formed next the pot, and sometimes toward the end of the boiling the porridge was lifted out of the pot bodily — so to speak — by the crust and served crust and all. Samp was pounded in a primitive and picturesque Indian mortar made of a hollowed block of wood, or the stump of a tree. The pestle was a heavy block of wood shaped like the interior of the mortar and fitted with a handle attached to one side. This block was fastened to the top of a growing sapling which gave it the required spring back after being pounded down on the corn. Pounding samp was slow work, often done in later years

IN OLD NEW YORK

by unskilled negroes and hence disparagingly termed "niggering" corn. After those simple mortars were abandoned elsewhere they were used on Long Island; and it was jestingly told that skippers in a fog could always get their bearings off the Long Island coast because they could hear the pounding of the samp-mortars.

Suppawn, another favorite of the settlers in New York, was an Indian dish made from Indian corn; it was a thick corn-meal and milk porridge. It soon was seen on every Dutch table, and is spoken of by all travellers in early New York.

From the gossiping pages of the Labadist preachers we find hints of good fare in Brooklyn in 1679: —

"Then was thrown upon the fire, to be roasted, a pail full of Gowanes oysters which are the best in the country. They are fully as good as those of England, better than those we eat at Falmouth. I had to try some of them raw. They are large and full, some of them not less than a foot long. Others are young and small. In consequence of the great quantities of them everybody keeps the shells for the burning of lime. They pickle the oysters in small casks and send them to Barbados. We had for supper a roasted haunch of venison which he had bought of the Indians for three guilders and a half of sea-want, that is fifteen stivers of Dutch money (fifteen cents), and which weighed thirty pounds. The meat was exceedingly tender and good and also quite fat. It had a slight aromatic flavor. We were also served with wild turkey, which was also fat and of a good flavor, and a wild goose, but that was rather dry. We saw here lying in a heap a whole hill of watermelons which were as large as pumpkins."

De Vries tells of an abundant supply of game in the colony; deer (as fat as any Holland deer can be); great wild turkeys, beautiful birds of golden bronze (one that he shot weighed thirty pounds); partridges and pigeons (in such great flocks that the sky was darkened). Domine Megapolensis says the plentiful wild turkeys and deer came to the hogpens of the Albany colonists to feed; fat Dutch swine and graceful red deer must have seemed strange trough companions. A stag was sold readily by an Indian for a jack-knife. In 1695 Rev. Mr. Miller said a quarter of venison could be bought "at your door" for ninepence. Wild swan came in plenty, "so that the bays and shores where they resort appear as if they were dressed in white drapery." Down the river swam hundreds of gray and white-headed geese nearly as stately as the swan; Van der Donck knew a gunner (and gives his name, Henry de Backer) who killed eleven gray geese with one shot from his gun. Gray ducks and pelicans were plentiful and cheap. Gone forever from the waters of New York are the beautiful gray ducks, white swan, gray geese, and pelican; anent these can we sigh for the good old times. The Earl of Strafford's letters and despatches, telling of the " Commodities of the Island called Maniti ore Long Ile wch is in the Continent of Virgenea," confirms all these reports and even tells of " fayre Turkees far greater than here, five hundred in a flocke," — which must have proved a noble sight.

The river was full of fish, and the bay; their plenty inspired the first poet of New Netherland to rhyming enumeration; among them were sturgeon — despised of Christians; and terrapin — not despised. " Some persons," wrote Van der Donck in 1656, " prepare delicious dishes from the water terrapin, which is luscious food." Two centuries and a half of appreciation pay equally warm tribute to the terrapin's reputation.

Patriarchal lobsters five and six feet long were in the bay. Van der Donck says "those a foot long are better for serving at table." Truly a lobster six feet long would seem a little awkward to serve. W. Eddis, in his "Letters from America" written in 1792, says these vast lobsters were caught in New York waters until Revolutionary days when "since the late incessant cannonading, they have entirely forsaken the coast; not one having been taken or seen since the commencement of hostilities." Crabs, too, were large, and some were "altogether soft." Van der Donck corroborates the foot-long oysters seen by the Labadists. He says the "large oysters roasted or stewed make a good bite," — a very good bite, it would seem.

Salted fish was as carefully prepared and amiably regarded in New York as in England and Holland at the same date. The ling and herring of the old country gave place in New York to shad. The greatest pains was taken in preparing, drying, and salting the plentiful shad. It is said that in towns, as in New York and Brooklyn, great heaps of shad were left when purchased at each door, and that the necessary cleaning and preparation was done on the street. As all housewives purchased shad and salted and packed at about the same time, those public scavengers, the domestic hogs, who roamed the town-streets unchecked (and ever welcomed), must have been specially useful at shad-time.

At a very early date apple-trees were set out and cultivated with much care and much success. Nowhere else, says Dankers, had he seen such fine apples. He notes the Double Paradise. The Newtown pippin, the Kingston spitzenburgh, the Poughkeepsie swaar-apple, the red-streak, guelderleng, and others of well-known name, show New York's attention to apple-raising. Kalm, the Swedish naturalist, spoke of the splendid apple-orchards throughout New York in 1749, and told of the horse-press for making cider. Cider soon rivalled in domestic use the beer of the Fatherland. It was constantly used during the winter season, and, diluted with water, sweetened, and flavored with nutmeg, made a grateful summer drink.

Peaches were in such lavish abundance as to become uncared for. The roads were covered with fallen peaches which even the ever-filled hogs would not eat. Plums were equally plentiful. Cherry-trees were planted in good numbers and produced in great quantities. "All travellers and passers-by could pick and eat at will," says Kalm. Comparatively scanty and poor are peaches, plums, and cherries in New York State to-day.

There were also plenty of vegetables: *cibollen* (chibbals), *peasen* (pease), *chicoreye* (chiccory), *karoten* (carrots), *artichock* (artichoke), *lattouwe* (lettuce), *beeten* (beets), *pastinaken* (parsnips), *radys* (radish), and many others. Pumpkins and squashes abounded, but do not appear to have been in as universal use as in New England. *Quaasiens* were so easily cooked "they were a favorite with the young women," says one authority; they "grew rapidly and digested well," also were qualities accorded in their favor. Under the name of *askutasquash*, or vine-apples, Roger Williams sung their praises. Musk-melons, water-melons, and cucumbers were grown in large number and excellent quality. Whether they cooked the *Duyvel's broodt*, the picturesque Dutch name for mushrooms, I know not, but the teeming woods of the Hudson valley offered them rich and abundant store of this dainty food.

The Swedish naturalist, Kalm, visited Albany in 1749. He has left to us a very full account of Albany food and fashions of serving at that time. He found the Albanians faring as did their great grandfathers in the Netherlands, who were sneeringly called "milk and cheese men," and he found them rasping their cheese as had their far-away forbears in Holland, and as do their descendants in Holland to this day. He writes thus: —

"The inhabitants of Albany are much more sparing than the English. The meat which is served up is often insufficient to satisfy the stomach, and the bowl does not circulate so freely as among the English. . . . Their meat and manner of dressing it is very different from that of the English. Their Breakfast is tea, commonly without milk. About thirty or forty years ago, tea was unknown to them, and they breakfasted either upon bread and butter or bread and milk. They never put sugar into the cup but put a small bit of it into their mouths while they drink. Along with the tea they eat bread and butter with slices of hung beef. Coffee is not usual here: they breakfast generally about seven. Their dinner is buttermilk and bread to which they sometimes add sugar, and then it is a delicious dish to them: or fresh milk and bread: or boiled or roasted flesh. They sometimes make use of buttermilk instead of fresh milk to boil a thin kind of porridge with, which tastes very sour but not disagreeable in hot weather. To each dinner they have a great salad prepared with abundance of vinegar and little or no oil. They frequently eat buttermilk, bread and salad, one mouthful after another. Their supper is generally bread and butter, or milk and bread. They sometimes eat cheese at breakfast and at dinner: it is not in slices but scraped or rasped so as to resemble coarse flour, which they pretend adds to the good taste of cheese. They commonly drink very small beer or pure water."

The " great salad dressed with vinegar" was doubtless " koolslaa," shredded cabbage, which we to-day call coleslaw. It was a universal dish also at that time in Holland. A woman-traveller there in 1756 wrote: —

" Everything of vivers is dear in Holland except vegetables, upon which the commons live all summer, and the better sort a great deall. Every body, great and small, sups on sallad with oil and vinegar."

The Dutch were famously fond of " bakers-meats," — all cakes and breads, — and excelled in making them, and made them in great variety. There was early legislation with regard to bakers, that they use just weights and good materials. In 1656 they were ordered to bake twice a week "both coarse and white loaves, both for Christians and Indians," at these prices: Fourteen stuyvers for a double coarse loaf of eight pounds, with smaller loaves at proportionate prices; and eight stuyvers for a white loaf of two pounds. Two years later the coarse wheat loaf of eight pounds was definitely priced at fourteen stuyvers in sea-want, ten in beavers, and seven in silver. The bakers complained, and a new assize of bread was established at a slightly higher rate. Under Dongan's charter bread-viewers were appointed; then the bread had to be marked with the baker's initials. I have puzzled over a prohibition of any bakers selling *koeckjes*, jumbles, and sweet cakes, unless he also had coarse bread for sale; and fancy it was that the extravagant and careless purchaser might not be tempted or forced to buy too costly food. One baker was prosecuted for having gingerbread in his window when he had no coarse bread. There were also "pye-women" as well as bakers.

COLONIAL DAYS

Favorite articles of food were three kinds of fried cakes of close kinship, thus described by Irving, — "the doughty doughnut, the tender olykoek, the crisp and crumbling cruller." The doughnut was an equal favorite in New England, and was in some localities called a simball, or simblin; which was a New England variant, a Puritan degradent of the simbling-cake, or simnel, of the English Mid-Lent Sunday. In New England country-houses doughnuts were eaten, indeed, are eaten, all the year around three meals a day; but Mrs. Vanderbilt says the Dutch in Flatbush only made them from November through January, because at that period the lard in which they were cooked was still fresh. She also says they were limited in their public appearance to the tea-table or for children to eat "between-meals." I don't know that I am willing to acquiesce in her assumption that when the Pilgrims were in Holland the English goodwives learned to make doughnuts from the Dutch *vrouws*, and thus be forced to yield doughnuts to the other triumphs of "Dutch colonial influence."

The famous *olykoeks*, or *olijkoecks*, were

thus concocted, as given by an old Dutch receipt of the year 1740 belonging to Mrs. Morris Patterson Ferris: —

"About twelve o'clock set a little yeast to rise, so as to be ready at five P. M. to mix with the following ingredients: $3\frac{3}{4}$ pounds of flour, 1 pound of sugar, $\frac{1}{2}$ pound of butter and lard mixed, $1\frac{1}{2}$ pints of milk, 6 eggs, 1 pint raised yeast. Warm the butter, sugar and milk together, grate a nutmeg in the flour, add eggs last. Place in a warm place to rise. If quite light at bedtime, work them down by pressing with the hand. At nine next morning make into small balls with the hand, and place in the centre of each a bit of raisin, citron, and apple chopped fine. Lay on a well-floured pie-board and allow them to rise again. They are frequently ready to boil at two o'clock. In removing them from the board use a knife, well-floured, and just give them a little roll with the hand to make them round. Have the fat boiling, and boil each one five minutes. When cool roll in sifted sugar."

The name means literally oil-cakes, and they were originally boiled or fried in oil. They were called "melting," and I am sure from this description of the process of manufacture they were delicate enough to deserve the appellation. The Hessian officers in

COLONIAL DAYS

Revolutionary times give eloquent approval of these "rich batter-cakes."

Tea-cakes which were made both in New England and New York were what Mrs. Vanderbilt calls "izer-cookies." They were so termed from the Dutch word *izer*, or *yser*, meaning iron; for they were baked in long-handled irons called wafer-irons, which often had the initials of the owners impressed in the metal, which impression of course rendered the letters in relief on the cakes. Often a date was also stamped on the irons. These wafer-irons sometimes formed part of a wedding outfit, having the initials of the bride and groom intertwined. The cakes were also called split-cakes because, thin as they were, often they were split and buttered before being eaten. Other wafer-cakes were called *oblyen*. Cinnamon-cakes resembled a delicate jumble with powdered cinnamon sprinkled on top. Puffards, or *puffertjes*, were eaten hot with powdered cinnamon and sugar, and were baked in a special pan, termed a puffet-pan. Wonders were flavored with orange peel and boiled in lard. Pork-cakes, made of chopped pork with spices, almonds, currants, raisins, and flavored with brandy, were a rich cake. The famous Schuyler wedding cake had among other ingredients, twelve dozen eggs, forty-eight pounds of raisins, twenty-four pounds of currants, four quarts of brandy, a quart of rum. This was mixed in a wash-tub.

Many of these cakes are now obsolete. In one of the old inventories of the Van Cortlandt family, in a list of kitchen utensils is the item, " 1 Bolly-byssha Pan." This is the Anglicized spelling of *bollo-bacia*, — *bolle* the old Dutch and Spanish word for a bun, or small loaf of flour and sugar; *bacia* the Spanish for a metal pan. In old receipts in the same family the word is called *bolla-bouche* and *bolla-buysies*. The receipt runs thus: —

"To a pound of flower a quarter of a pound of sugar, the same of butter, 4 egs, sum Nut-Meg and Senamond, milk & yeast, A pint of milk to 2 pound of flower."

Domestic swine afforded the Dutch many varied and appetizing foods. Two purely Dutch dishes were *rolliches* and head cheese. *Rolliches* were made of lean beef and fat cut in pieces about as large as dice, then highly seasoned with herbs and spices, sewed in tripe and boiled for several hours. This roll was then pressed into an oblong loaf, which made pretty slices when cut and served cold. Head cheese, or *hoofd-kaas*, was similar in appearance, but was made of pigs'-feet and portions of the head chopped fine, boiled in a bag, and pressed into the shape of a cheese. This also was served in cold slices.

Speck ende kool, pork and cabbage, was another domestic stand-by; fried pork and apples were made into an appetizing dinner dish. Roast ducks were served with pork-dumplings, — of which the mystery of manufacture is unknown to me.

A great favorite of the Dutch is shown through this advertisement in the "New York Gazette" of December 17, 1750: —

"The Printer hereof, ever mindful to please and gratify his Customers, finding but little Entertainment at present suitable to the Genius of many; has been obliged to provide for the Winter Evening Diversion of such of his Friends as are that way inclined, A Parcel of the Nuts commonly called KESKATOMAS NUTS which he sells at *One Shilling* per Half a Peck. N. B. They are all right 'Sopus and of the right sort.'"

A writer in the "Literary World" in 1850 thus defines and eulogizes these nuts: —

> "Hickory, shell-bark, kiskitomas nut!
> Or whatsoever thou art called, thy praise
> Has ne'er been sounded yet in poet's lays."

Michaux, in his "North American Sylva," says that many descendants of the Dutch in New Jersey and New York still call the hickory-nut *Kisky-Thomas-nuts*. The name is derived from an Indian word, not from the Dutch. These nuts were served at every winter evening company, great or small. Mrs. Grant tells of their appearance on the tea-table.

Of the drinking habits of the Dutch colonists I can say that they were those of all the colonies, — excessive. Tempered in their tastes somewhat by the universal brewing and drinking of beer, they did not use as much rum as the Puritans of New England, nor drink as deeply as the Virginia planters; but the use of liquor was universal. A libation was poured on every transaction, every action, at every happening in the community, in public life as well as in private. John Barleycorn was ever a witness at the drawing up of a contract, the signing of a deed, the selling of a farm, the purchase of goods, the arbitration of a suit. If either party to a contract "backed out" before signing, he did not back away from the "treat," but had to furnish half a barrel of beer or a gallon of rum to assuage the pangs of disappointment. Liquor was served at auctions or "vendues" free, so Madam Knight says,— buyers becoming expansive in bidding when well primed. It appeared at weddings, funerals, church-openings, deacon-ordainings, and house-raisings. No farm hand in hayingfield, no sailor on a vessel, no workman in a mill, no cobbler, tailor, carpenter, mason, or tinker would work without some strong drink, some treat. The bill for liquor where many workmen were employed, as in a house-raising, was often a heavy one.

A detailed example of the imperative furnishing of liquor to workmen is found in the contracts and bills for building in 1656 the first stone house erected at Albany, a government house or fort. It cost 12,213 guilders in wampum, or about $3,500, and was built under the charge of Jan de la Montagne, the Vice-Director of the Fort. Every step in the erection of this building was taken knee-deep in liquor. The dispensing of drink began when the old wooden fort was levelled; a tun of strong beer was furnished to the pullers-down. At the laying of the first stones of the wall a case of brandy, an anker (thirty-three quarts) of brandy, and thirty-two guilders' worth of other liquor wet the thirsty whistles of the masons. When the cellar beams were laid, the carpenters had their turn. Two barrels of strong beer, three cases of brandy, and seventy-two florins' worth of small beer rested them temporarily from their labors. When the second tier of beams was successfully in place, the carpenters had two more cases of brandy and a barrel of beer.

The beams had already received a previous "wetting;" for when brought to the building they had been left without the wall, and had been carried within, one at a time, by eight men who had half a barrel of beer for each beam. There were thirty-three beams in all.

All the wood-carriers, teamsters, carpenters, stone-cutters, and masons had, besides these special treats, a daily dram of a gill of brandy apiece, and three pints of beer at dinner. They were dissatisfied, and "solicited" another pint of beer. Even the carters who brought wood and the boatmen who floated down spars were served with liquor. When the carpenters placed the roof-tree, a half-barrel of liquor was given them. Another half-barrel under the name of tiles-beer went to the tile-setters. The special completion of the winding staircase demanded five guilders' worth of liquor. When the house was finished, a *kraeg*, or housewarming, of both food and drink to all the workmen and their wives was demanded and refused. Well it might be refused, when the liquor bill without it amounted to seven hundred and sixteen guilders.

The amount of liquor required to help in conducting an election was very great. In 1738 James Alexander and Eventhus Van Horne paid over seventy-two pounds for one election bill. Liquor then was cheap. This sum purchased sixty-two gallons of Jamaica rum, several gallons of brandy, eight gallons of lime-juice, a " pyd " of wine which cost sixteen pounds (I don't know what a " pyd " could have been), a large amount of shrub, and mugs and " gugs" and " bottels." There were also two bagpipes and a fiddler.

IN OLD NEW YORK

Let me give, as a feeble excuse for the large consumption of beer, cider, etc., that the water was poor in many of the towns. Kalm wrote of the Albany water:—

"The water of several of the wells was very cool about this time, but had a kind of acid taste which was not very agreeable. I think this water is not very wholesome for people who are not used to it. Nearly every house in Albany has its well, the water of which is applied to common use; but for tea, brewing, and washing they commonly take the water of the river."

What can be the other "common use" to which well-water was applied, except putting out fires,—which is an infrequent use?

In New York City the water was equally poor. The famous Tea-water Pump supplied in barrels for many years the more fastidious portion of the community. Perhaps we could scarcely expect them to drink much water when they had to buy it.

Our notions of life in New Netherland have been so thoroughly shaped by Diedrich Knickerbocker's tergiversating account thereof, that it would be difficult for us to make any marked change in the picture he has painted. Nor do we need to do so. For though the details of public and official life and characters in that day have been wilfully distorted by Irving's keen humor, still the atmosphere of his picture is undeniably correct, and the domestic life he has shown us was the life of that colony. I find nothing, after much illumination through careful examination of old records and the contemporary accounts given by early travellers, to change in any considerable degree the estimate of every-day life in New Netherland which I gained from Irving, save in one respect, — the account of Dutch table manners, and the attributing to the Dutch burghers of lax hospitality at dinner-time, which I cannot believe. Madam Knight wrote of her New York hosts in 1704: —

"They are sociable to one another, and Curteos and Civill to Strangers, and fare well in their houses. . . . They are sociable to a degree, their tables being as free to their Naybours as themselves."

Mrs. Grant, writing of Albanians half a century later, gives a detailed description of their manners as hosts, which might serve as an explanation of apparent inhospitality in the time of Walter the Doubter: —

"They were exceedingly social, and visited each other very frequently, beside the regular assembling together in porches every fine evening. Of the more substantial luxuries of the table they knew little, and of the formal and ceremonious parts of good breeding still less.

"If you went to spend a day anywhere, you were received in a manner we should think very cold. No one rose to welcome you; no one wondered you had not come sooner, or apologized for any deficiency in your entertainment. Dinner, which was very early, was served exactly in the same manner as if there were only the family. The house, indeed, was so exquisitely neat and well regulated, that you could not surprise them; and they saw each other so often and so easily that intimates made no difference. Of strangers they were shy; not by any means from want of hospitality, but from a consciousness that people who had little to value themselves on but their knowledge of the modes and ceremonies of polished life disliked their sincerity and despised their simplicity. If you showed no insolent wonder, but easily and quietly adopted their manners, you would receive from them not only very great civility, but much essential kindness. . . . After sharing this plain and unceremonious dinner, which might, by the bye, chance to be a very good one, but was invariably that which was meant for the family, tea was served in at a very early hour. And here it was that the distinction shown to strangers commenced. Tea here was a perfect 'regale,' accompanied by various sorts of cake unknown to us, cold pastry, and great quantities of sweetmeats and preserved fruits of various kinds, and plates of hickory and other nuts ready cracked. In all manner of confectionery and pastry these people excelled; and having fruit in great abundance, which cost them nothing, and getting sugar home at an easy rate, in return for their exports to the West Indies, the quantity of these articles used in families, otherwise plain and frugal, was astonishing. Tea was never unaccompanied with some of these petty articles; but for strangers a great display was made. If you stayed supper, you were sure of a most substantial though plain one. In this meal they departed, out of compliment to the strangers, from their usual simplicity. Having dined between twelve and one, you were quite prepared for it. You had either game or poultry roasted, and always shell-fish in the season; you had also fruit in abundance. All this with much neatness, but no form. The seeming coldness with which you were first received wore off by degrees."

It may be noted that Mrs. Grant gives a very different notion of Albany fare than does Kalm, already quoted; and she wrote scarce a score of years after his account. She tells — in this extract — not of wealthy folk, though they were truly gentle-folk, if simplicity of living, kindliness, and good sense added in many cases to good birth could make these plain Albanians gentle-folk. And in truth it seems to me a cheerful picture, — one of true though shy hospitality; pleasant of contemplation in our days of formality and extravagance of entertaining, of scant knowledge of the true home life even of those we call our friends.

CHAPTER VIII

THE DUTCH VROUWS

THERE is much evidence to show that the women of Dutch descent of the early years of New Netherland and New York had other traits than those of domestic housewifery; they partook frequently of the shrewdness and business sagacity and capacity of their Dutch husbands. Widows felt no hesitation and experienced no difficulty in carrying on the business affairs of their dead partners; wives having capable, active husbands boldly engaged in independent business operations of their own; their ventures were as extended and fearless as those of the men. They traded for peltries with the Indians with marked success. I suspect part of the profit may have come through the Indian braves' serene confidence in their own superior sagacity in bargaining and trafficking with the "white squaws." The Labadist travellers wrote thus despitefully of a "female-trader" in Albany in 1679: —

"This woman, although not of openly godless life, is more wise than devout, although her knowledge is not very extensive, and does not surpass that of the women of New Netherland. She is a truly worldly woman, proud and conceited, and sharp in trading with *wild* people as well as *tame* ones, or what shall I call them not to give them the name of Christians, or if I do, it is only to distinguish them from the others. She has a husband, who is her second one. He remains at home quietly while she travels over the country to carry on the trading. In fine, she is one of the Dutch female-traders who understand the business so well. If these be the persons who are to make Christians of the heathen, what will the latter be?"

Certain traits of a still more influential and widely known female-trader in New Netherland are shown to us in Dankers' pages through slight but extremely vivid side-lights, but which (having been written on shipboard) may perhaps be taken with the grain of palliative salt which should frequently be cast upon the condemnatory utterances of sea-weary, if not sea-sick, passengers on the raging deep when they regard everything connected with the odious ship which confines them. We are introduced to this colonial woman of affairs in the sub-title of the journal, which states that the journey to New Netherland was made "in a small Flute-ship called the Charles, of which Thomas Singleton was Master; but the superior Authority over both Ship and Cargo was in Margaret Filipse, who was the Owner of both, and with whom we agreed for our Passage from Amsterdam to New York, in New Netherland, at seventy-five Guilders for each Person, payable in Holland."

This "Margaret Filipse" was the daughter of Adolph Hardenbrook who settled in Bergen, opposite New Amsterdam. She was the widow of the merchant trader Peter Rudolphus De Vries when she married Frederick Philipse. Her second husband was a carpenter by trade, who worked for Governor Stuyvesant; but on his marriage with the wealthy Widow De Vries, he became her capable business partner, and finally was counted the richest man in the colony. She owned ships running to many ports, and went repeatedly to Holland in her own ships as supercargo. She was visited by Dankers in Amsterdam in June, 1679. According to the custom of his religious sect, he always called her by her Christian name, and wrote of her as Margaret. He says: —

"We spoke to Margaret, inquiring of her when the ship would leave. She answered she had given orders to have everything in readiness to sail to-day, but she herself was of opinion it would not be before Monday. We offered her the money to pay for our passage, but she refused to receive it at that time, saying she was tired and could not be troubled with it that day."

They waited patiently on shipboard for several days for Madam Philipse to embark, and at last he writes: —

"We were all very anxious for Margaret to arrive, so that we might not miss a good wind. Jan and some of the other passengers were much dissatisfied. Jan declared, 'If this wind blows over I will write her a letter that will make her ears tingle.'"

Landing at an English port, the travellers bought wine and vinegar, "for we began to see it would go slim with us on the voyage," and Margaret bought a ship which was made ready to go to the Isle of May and then to the Barbadoes. Over the purchase and equipment of this ship arose a great quarrel, for "those miserable, covetous people Margaret and her husband" tried to take away the Charles' long-boat because timber for a new one was cheaper in New York than in Falmouth, England. Naturally, the passengers objected to crossing the Atlantic without a ship's-boat. Dankers complained further of Margaret's "miserable covetousness," — that she made the ship lay to for an hour and a half and sent out the jolly-boat to pick up a ship's mop or swab worth six cents; and the carpenter swore because she had not furnished new leather and spouts for the pumps. Dankers explained at length the enhancement of the Philipse profits through some business arrangement and preferment with the Governor, by which Frederick Philipse became the largest trader with the Five Nations at Albany, had a profitable slave-trade with Africa, and, it is asserted, was in close bonds with the Madagascar pirates. Whether "Margaret" favored this trade with the pirates is not known; but it could probably be said of her trade, as of many others in the colony, that it was hard to draw the dividing line between privateering and piracy.

Her calling was not singular in New Amsterdam. The little town abounded in women-traders.

Elizabeth Van Es was the daughter of one of the early Albany magistrates. She married Gerrit Bancker, and on becoming a widow removed to New York, where she promptly opened a store on her own account, and conducted it with success till her death, in 1694. In the inventory of her effects were a share in a brigantine, a large quantity of goods and peltries, as well as various silver-clasped Bibles, gold and stone rings, and silver tankards and beakers, showing her success in her business career. The wife of the great Jacob Leisler, a Widow Vanderveen when he married her, was a trader. Lysbet, the widow of Merchant Reinier, became the wife of Domine Drisius, of New York. She carried on for many years a thriving trade on what is now Pearl Street, near Whitehall Street, and was known to every one as Mother Drisius. The wife of Domine Van Varick also kept a small store, and thus helped out her husband's salary.

Heilke Pieterse was the wife of the foremost blacksmith of New Amsterdam; and as he monopolized the whole business of Long Island, he died very rich, — worth at least ten thousand dollars. Not overwhelmed or puffed up with the inheritance of such opulence, Heilke carried on her husband's business for many years with success.

Margaret Backer was another successful business woman. For years she acted as attorney for her husband while he was in foreign countries attending to that end of his great foreign trade. Rachel Vinje, involved in heavy lawsuits over the settlement of an estate, pleaded her own case in court, and was successful. Women were constant in their appearance in court as parties in contracts and agreements.

The Schuyler family did not lack examples of stirring women-kind. Margaret van Schlictenhorst, wife of the first Peter Schuyler, being left a widow, managed her husband's estate in varied business lines with such thrift and prudence that in her will, made at eighty years of age, she could assert that the property had vastly increased. She was not out of public affairs, for during the Leisler troubles she was the second largest subscriber to the fund in support of the government; and she also lent money to pay the borrowed soldiers. Her niece, Heligonda van Schlictenhorst, a shrewd spinster, was a merchant, and furnished public supplies. The daughter of Peter Schuyler married John Collins. A letter of his, dated 1722, shows her capacity. I quote a clause from it: —

"Since you left us my wife has been in the Indian country, and Van Slyck had purchased what he could at the upper end of the land; she purchased the rest from Ignosedah to his purchase. She has gone through a great deal of hardship and trouble about it, being from home almost ever since you left us; and prevailed with the Indians whilst there with trouble and expense to mark out the land where the mine is into the woods. Mrs. Feathers has been slaving with her all this while, and hard enough to do with that perverse generation, to bring them to terms."

The picture of these two women in the wilds, treating and bargaining and trading with the savages, seems curious enough to us to-day. Women seem to have excelled in learning the Indian languages. The daughter of Anneke Jans was the best interpreter in the colony, and served as interpreter to

Stuyvesant during his famous treaty with the Six Nations.

Many of the leading taverns or hostelries were kept by women, — a natural calling, certainly, for good housewives. Madam Van Borsum was mistress of the Ferry Tavern in Breucklen. Annetje Litschar kept the tavern which stood near the present site of Hanover Square. Metje Wessell's hostelry stood on the north side of Pearl Street, near Whitehall Street.

More successful still and bold in trade was Widow Maria Provoost. Scarce a ship came into port from Holland, England, the Mediterranean, West Indies, or the Spanish Main, but brought to her large consignments of goods. Her Dutch business correspondence was a large one. She, too, married a second time, and, as Madam James Alexander, filled a most dignified position, and became the mother of Lord Stirling.

In a letter written by her husband, James Alexander, to his brother William, and dated October 21, 1721, there is found a passage which gives extraordinary tribute to her business capacity and her powers of endurance alike. It reads thus: —

"Two nights agoe at eleven o'clock, my wife was Brought to bed of a Daughter and is in as good health as can be Expected, and does more than can be Expected of any woman, for till within a few hours of her being brought to bed She was in her Shop, and ever Since has given the price of Goods to her prentice, who comes to her and asks it when Customers come in. The very next day after She was brought to bed she Sold goods to above thirty pounds value. And here the business matters of her Shop which is Generally Esteemed the best in New York, she with a prentice of about 16 years of age perfectly well manages without the Least help from me, you may guess a little of her success."

He closes his letter with a eulogy which can be cordially endorsed by every reader:

"I must say my fortune in America is above my Expectation, and I think even my Deserts, and the greatest of my good fortune is in getting so Good a Wife as I have, who alone would make ae man easy and happy had he nothing else to depend on."

Madam Alexander accumulated great wealth, and spent it handsomely. She was the only person in town, besides the Governor, who kept a coach. Her will is an interesting document, and shows a fine style of housekeeping. The enumeration of great and lesser drawing-rooms, front and back parlors, blue and gold leather room, green and gold leather room, tapestry room, chintz room, etc., show its pretension and extent. She lived on Broad Street, had a fine garden laid out in the Dutch taste, a house full of servants, and spent her money freely as she made it thriftily. A very good portrait of her exists. It shows an interesting countenance, with fine features, a keen eye, and indicating robust health. She is not dressed with great elegance, wearing the costume of the day, — a commonplace frilled cap, folded kerchief, close sleeves, such as we are familiar with in portraits of English women of her time.

Jane Colden, the daughter of Governor Cadwallader Colden, was of signal service, not in trade, but in science. A letter written by her father explains her interest and usefulness: —

"Botany is an amusement which may be made agreeable to the ladies who are often at a loss to fill up their time. Their natural curiosity and the pleasure they take in the beauty and variety of dress seem to fit them for it.

"I have a daughter who has an inclination to reading, and a curiosity for Natural Philosophy or Natural History, and a sufficient curiosity for attaining a competent knowledge. I took the pains to explain Linnæus' system, and to put it into an English form for her use by freeing it from technical terms, which was easily done, by using two or three words in the place of one. She is now grown very fond of the study, and has made such a progress in it as, I believe, would please you, if you saw her performance. Though she could not have been persuaded to learn the terms at first, she now understands to some degree Linnæus' characters, — notwithstanding she does not understand Latin. She has already a pretty large volume in writing of the description of plants. She has shewn a method of taking the impression of the leaves on paper with printers' ink, by a simple kind of rolling press which is of use in distinguishing the species. No description in words alone, can give so clear an idea, as when assisted with a picture. She has the impression of three hundred plants in the manner you'll see by the samples. That you may have some conception of her performance, and her manner of describing, I propose to enclose some samples in her own writing, some of which I think are new genera."

Peter Collinson said she was the first lady to study the Linnæan system, and deserved to have her name celebrated; and John Ellis, writing of her to Linnæus in 1758, asks that a genus be named, for her, Coldenella. She was also a correspondent of Dr. Whyte of Edinburgh, and many learned societies in Europe. Walter Rutherfurd enumerates her talents, and caps them with a glowing tribute to her cheese-making.

We find the women of the times full of interest in public affairs and active in good works. In the later days of the province, we learn of the gifts to the army at Crown Point in 1755. In those days the generous farmers of Queens County, Long Island, collected one thousand and fifteen sheep, and these were "cheerfully given."

"While their husbands at Great Neck were employed in getting sheep, the good mothers in that neighborhood in a few hours collected nearly seventy good large cheeses, and sent them to New York to be forwarded with the sheep to the army." Kings County defrayed the expense of conveying these sheep and cheeses to the army; and a letter of gratitude was promptly returned by the commander-in-chief, Sir William Johnson, who said, —

"This generous humanity is unanimously and gratefully applauded here by all. We pray that your benevolence may be returned to you by the great Shepherd of the human kind a thousand fold. And may those amiable housewives to whose skill we owe the refreshing cheeses long continue to shine in their useful and endearing stations."

Kings County and Suffolk also sent cheeses, and we learn also: —

"The Women of County Suffolk ever good in such Occasions are knitting several large bags of stockings and mittens to be sent to the poorer soldiers at Forts William Henry and Edward."

In studying the history of the province, I am impressed with the debt New Yorkers of Dutch descent owe, not to their forefathers, but to their foremothers; the conspicuous decorum of life of these women and their great purity of morals were equalled by their good sense and their wonderful capacity in both domestic and public affairs. They were as good patriots as they were good business women; and though they were none of them what Carlyle calls "writing-women," it was not from poverty of good sense or natural intelligence, but simply from the imperfection of their education through lack of good and plentiful schools, and also want of stimulus owing to absence of literary atmosphere.

A very shrewd woman-observer, writing in the middle of the eighteenth century of the Dutch, gives what seems to me a very just estimate and good description of one of their traits. She says: "Though they have no vivacity, they are smarter, a great deal smarter, than the English, that is, more *uptaking*." Those who know the exact Scotch meaning of "uptaking," which is somewhat equivalent to Anthony Trollope's "observation and reception," will understand the closeness of the application of the term to the Dutch.

The Dutch women especially were "uptaking;" adaptive of all comfort-bringing methods of housekeeping. This was noted by Guicciardini in Holland as early as 1563. They were far advanced in knowledge and execution of healthful household conditions, through their beautiful cleanliness. Irving says very truthfully of them: "In those good days of simplicity and sunshine a passion for cleanliness was the leading principle in domestic economy, and the universal test of a good housewife." Kalm says: "They are almost over nice and cleanly in regard to the floor, which is frequently scoured twice a week." They found conditions of housekeeping entirely changed in America, but the passionate love of cleanliness fostered in the Fatherland clung long in their hearts. Their "Œconomy" and thrift were also beautiful.

An advertisement in the "New York Gazette" of April 1, 1751, shows that the thrift of the community lingered until Revolutionary times:—

"Elizabeth Boyd gives notice that she will as usual graft Pieces in knit Jackets and Breeches not to be discern'd, also to graft and foot Stockings, and Gentlemens Gloves, mittens or Muffatees made out of old Stockings, or runs them in the Heels. She likewise makes Childrens Stockings out of Old Ones."

Other dames taught more elegant accomplishments:—

"Martha Gazley, now in the city of New York, Makes and Teacheth the following curious Works, viz.: Artificial Fruit and Flowers and other Wax-Work, Nun's Work, Philligree and Pencil-work upon Muslin, all sorts of Needlework, and Raising of Paste, as also to Paint upon Glass, and Transparent for Sconces with other Works. If any young Gentlewomen, or others, are inclined to learn any or all of the above-mentioned curious Works, they may be carefully taught and instructed in the same by said Martha Gazley."

Mrs. Van Cortlandt, in her delightful account of home-life in Westchester County, says of the industrious Dutch women and their accomplishments and occupations: —

" Knitting was an art much cultivated, the Dutch women excelling in the variety and intricacy of the stitches. A knitting sheath, which might be of silver or of a homely goose-quill, was an indispensable utensil, and beside it hung the ball-pincushion. Crewel-work and silk embroidery were fashionable, and surprisingly pretty effects were produced. Every little maiden had her sampler, which she began with the alphabet and numerals following them with a Scriptural text or verse of a metrical psalm. Then fancy was let loose on birds, beasts, and trees. Most of the old families possessed framed pieces of embroidery, the handiwork of female ancestors. Flounces and trimmings for aprons worked with delicately tinted silks on muslin were common. I have several yards of fine muslin painted in the early days with full-blown thistles in the appropriate colors.

Fringe looms were in use, and cotton and silk fringes were woven."

Tape-looms were also found in many households; and the weaving of tapes and "none-so-prettys" was deemed very light and elegant work.

Though to the Dutch is ascribed the invention of the thimble, I never think of the Dutch women as excelling in fine needlework; and I note that the teachers of intricate and novel embroidery-stitches are always Englishwomen; but in turn the English goodwives must yield to the Dutch the palm of comfortable, attractive housewifery, as well as shrewd, untiring business capacity.

CHAPTER IX

THE COLONIAL WARDROBE

THE Dutch goodwife worked hard from early morn till sunset. She worked in restricted ways, she had few recreations and pleasures and altogether little variety in her life; but she possessed what doubtless proved to her in that day, as it would to any woman in this day, a source of just satisfaction, a soothing to the spirit, a staying of melancholy, a moral support second only to the solace of religion, — namely, a large quantity of very good clothes, which were substantial, cheerful, and suitable, if not elegant.

The Dutch never dressed "in a plaine habbit according to the maner of a poore wildernesse people," as the Connecticut colonists wrote of themselves to Charles II.; nor were they weary wanderers in a wilderness as were Connecticut folk.

IN OLD NEW YORK

I have not found among the statutes of New Netherland any sumptuary laws such as were passed in Connecticut, Massachusetts, and Virginia, to restrain and attempt to prohibit luxury and extravagance in dress. Nor have I discovered in the court-records any evidences of magisterial reproof of finery; there is, on the contrary, much indirect proof of encouragement to "dress orderly and well according to the fashion and the time." Of course the Dutch had no Puritanical dread of over-rich garments; and we must also never forget New Netherland was not under the control of a government nor of a religious band, but of a trading-company.

The ordinary dress of the fair dames and damsels of New Amsterdam has been vividly described by Diedrich Knickerbocker; and even with the additional light upon their wardrobe thrown by the lists contained in colonial inventories, I still think his description of their every-day dress exceedingly good for one given by a man. He writes:

"Their hair, untortured by the abominations of art, was scrupulously pomatumed back from their foreheads with a candle, and covered with a little cap of quilted calico, which fitted exactly to their heads. Their petticoats of linsey-woolsey were striped with a variety of gorgeous dyes, though I must confess those gallant garments were rather short, scarce reaching below the knee; but then they made up in the number, which generally equalled that of the gentlemen's small-clothes; and what is still more praiseworthy, they were all of their own manufacture, — of which circumstance, as may well be supposed, they were not a little vain.

"Those were the honest days, in which every woman stayed at home, read the Bible, and wore pockets, — ay, and that, too, of a goodly size, fashioned with patchwork into many curious devices, and ostentatiously worn on the outside. These, in fact, were convenient receptacles where all good housewives carefully stored away such things as they wished to have at hand; by which means they often came to be incredibly crammed.

"Besides these notable pockets, they likewise wore scissors and pincushions suspended from their girdles by red ribbons, or, among the more opulent and showy classes, by a brass and even silver chains, indubitable tokens of thrifty housewives and industrious spinsters. I cannot say much in vindication of the shortness of the petticoats; it doubtless was introduced for the purpose of giving the stockings a chance to be seen, which were generally of blue worsted, with magnificent red clocks; or perhaps to display a well-turned ankle and a neat though serviceable foot, set off by a high-heeled leathern shoe, with a large and splendid silver buckle.

"There was a secret charm in those petticoats, which no doubt entered into the consideration of the prudent gallants. The wardrobe of a lady was in those days her only fortune; and she who had a good stock of petticoats and stockings was as absolutely an heiress as is a Kamtschatka damsel with a store of bear-skins, or a Lapland belle with plenty of reindeer."

A Boston lady, Madam Knights, visiting New York in 1704, wrote: —

"The English go very fashionable in their dress. But the Dutch, especially the middling sort, differ from our women, in their habitt go loose, wear French muches wch are like a Capp and head-band in one, leaving their ears bare, which are sett out with jewells of a large size and many in number; and their fingers hoop't with rings, some with large stones in them of many Coullers, as were their pendants in their ears, which you should see very old women wear as well as Young."

This really gives a very good picture of the *vrouws;* "loose in their habit," wearing sacques and loose gowns, not laced in with pointed waists as were the English and Boston women; with the ornamental headdress, and the gay display of stoned earrings and rings, which was also not the usual wear of New England women, who generally owned only a few funeral rings.

In the inventories of personal estates contained in the Surrogate's Court we find details of the wardrobe; but as I have enumerated and defined all the different articles at some length in my book, "Costume of Colonial Times," I will not repeat the definitions here; but it should be remembered that in the enumeration of the articles of clothing, many stuffs and materials of simple names were often of exceedingly good and even rich quality. From those inventories we have proof that all Dutch women had plenty of clothes; while the wives of the burgomasters, the opulent merchants, and those in authority, had rich clothes. I have given in full in my book a list of the clothing of a wealthy New York dame, Madam De Lange; but I wish to refer to it again as an example of a really beautiful wardrobe. In it were twelve petticoats of varying elegance, some worth two pounds fifteen shillings each, which would be more than fifty dollars to-day. They were of silk lined with silk, striped stuff, scarlet cloth, and ash-gray cloth. Some were trimmed with gold lace. With those petticoats were worn samares and samares-a-potoso, six in number, which were evidently jackets or fancy bodies; these were of calico, crape, "tartanel," and silk. One trimmed with lace was worth three pounds. Waistcoats and bodies also appear; also fancy sleeves. Love-hoods of silk and cornet-caps with lace make a pretty headgear to complete this costume, with which was worn the reim or silver girdle with hanging purse, and also with a handsome number of diamond, amber, and white coral jewels.

The colors in the Dutch gowns were almost uniformly gay, — in keen contrast to the sad-colored garments of New England. Madam Cornelia de Vos in a green cloth petticoat, a red and blue "Haarlamer" waistcoat, a pair of red and yellow sleeves, and a purple "Pooyse" apron was a blooming flower-bed of color.

The dress of Vrouentje Ides Stoffelsen, a very capable Dutchwoman who went to Bergen Point to live, varied a little from that of these town dames. Petticoats she had, and waistcoats, bodies and sleeves; but there was also homelier attire, — purple and blue aprons, four pairs of pattens, a fur cap instead of love-hoods, and twenty-three caps. She wore the simpler and more universal head-gear, — a close linen or calico cap.

The head covering was of considerable importance in New Amsterdam, as it was in Holland as well as in England at that date. We find that it was also costly. In 1665 Mistress Piertje Jans sold a fine "little ornamental headdress" for fifty-five guilders to the young daughter of Evert Duyckinck. But it seems that Missy bought this "genteel head-clothes" without the knowledge or permission of her parents, and on its arrival at the Duyckinck home Vrouw Duyckinck promptly sent back the emblem of extravagance and disobedience. Summoned to court by the incensed milliner who wished no rejected head-dresses on her hands, and who claimed that the transaction was from the beginning with full cognizance of the parents, Father Duyckinck pronounced the milliner's bill extortionate; and furthermore said gloomily, with a familiar nineteenth-century phraseology of New York fathers, that "this was no time to be buying and wearing costly head-dresses." But the court decided in the milliner's favor.

It is to be deplored that we have no fashion-plates of past centuries to show to us in exact presentment the varying modes worn by New York dames from year to year; that method of fashion-conveying has been adopted but a century. The modes in olden days travelled from country to country, from town to town, in the form of dolls or "babies," as they were called, wearing miniature model costumes. These dolls were dressed by cutters and tailors in Paris or London, and with various tiny modish garments were sent out on their important mission across the water. In Venice a doll attired in the last fashions — the toilette of the year — was for centuries exhibited on each Ascension Day at the "Merceria" for the edification of noble Venetian dames, who eagerly flocked to the attractive sight. Not less eagerly did American dames flock to provincial mantua-makers and milliners to see the London-dressed babies with their miniature garments. Even in this century, fashions were brought to New York and Philadelphia and Albany through "milliners' boxes" containing dressed dolls. Mrs. Vanderbilt tells of one much admired fashion-doll of her youth who had a treasured old age as a juvenile goddess.

A leading man of New Amsterdam, a burgomaster, had at the time of his death, near the end of Dutch rule, this plentiful number of substantial garments: a cloth coat with silver buttons, a stuff coat, cloth breeches, a cloth coat with gimp buttons, a black cloth coat, a silk coat, breeches and doublet, a silver cloth breeches and doublet, a velvet waistcoat with silver lace, a buff coat with silk sleeves, three "gross-green" cloaks, several old suits of clothes, linen, hosiery, silver-buckled shoes, an ivory-headed cane, and a hat. One hat may seem very little with so many other garments; but the real beaver hats of those days were so substantial, so well-made, so truly worthy an article of attire, that they could be constantly worn and yet last for years. They were costly; some were worth several pounds apiece.

Gayer masculine garments are told of in other inventories: green silk breeches flowered with silver and gold, silver gauze breeches, yellow fringed gloves, lacquered hats, laced shirts and neck-cloths, and (towards the end of the century, and nearly through the eighteenth century) a vast variety of wigs. For over a hundred years these unnatural abominations, which bore no pretence of resembling the human hair, often in grotesque, clumsy, cumbersome shapes, bearing equally fantastic names, and made of various indifferent and coarse materials, loaded the heads and lightened the pockets of our ancestors. I am glad to note that they were taxed by the government of the province of New York. The barber and wig-maker soon became a very important personage in a community so given over to costly modes of dressing the head. Advertisements in the newspapers show the various kinds of wigs worn in the middle of the eighteenth century. From the "New York Gazette" of May 9, 1737, we learn of a thief's stealing "one gray Hair Wig, one Horse hair wig not the worse for wearing, one Pale Hair Wig, not worn five times, marked V. S. E., one brown Natural wig, One old wig of goat's hair put in buckle." Buckle meant to curl; and derivatively a wig was in

COLONIAL DAYS

buckle when it was rolled on papers for curling. Other advertisements tell of "Perukes, Tets, and Fox-tails after the Genteelest Fashion. Ladies' Tets and wigs in perfect imitation of their own hair." Other curious notices are of "Orange Butter" for "Gentlewomen to comb up their hair with."

This use of orange butter as a pomatum was certainly unique; it was really a Dutch marmalade. I read in my "Closet of Rarities," dated 1706: —

"The Dutch Way to make Orange-butter. Take new cream two gallons, beat it up to a thicknesse, then add half a pint of orange-flower-water, and as much red wine, and so being become the thicknesse of butter it has both the colour and smell of an orange."

A very characteristic and eye-catching advertisement was this from the "New York Gazette" of May 21, 1750: —

"This is to acquaint the Public, that there is lately arrived from London the Wonder of the World, *an Honest* Barber and Peruke Maker, who might have worked for the King, if his Majesty would have employed him: It was not for the want of Money he came here, for he had enough of that at Home, nor for the want of Business,

that he advertises hinself, BUT to acquaint the Gentlemen and Ladies, That *Such a Person is now in Town*, living near *Rosemary Lane* where Gentlemen and Ladies may be supplied with Goods as follows, viz.: Tyes, Full-Bottoms, Majors, Spencers, Fox-Tails, Ramalies, Tacks, cut and bob Perukes: Also Ladies Tatematongues and Towers after the Manner that is now wore at Court. *By their Humble and Obedient Servant,*
"JOHN STILL."

With the change from simple Dutch ways of hairdressing came in other details more constrained modes of dressing. With the wig-maker came the stay-maker, whose curious advertisements may be read in scores in the provincial newspapers; and his arbitrary fashions bring us to modern times.

From the deacons' records of the Dutch Reformed Church at Albany we catch occasional hints of the dress of the children of the Dutch colonists. There was no poorhouse, and few poor; but since the church occasionally helped worthy folk who were not rich, we find the deacons in 1665 and 1666 paying for blue linen for *schorteldoecykers*, or aprons, for Albany *kindeken;* also for *haaken en oogen*, or hooks and eyes, for warm under-waists called *borsrockyen*. They bought linen for *luyers*, which were neither pinning-blankets nor diapers, but a sort of swaddling clothes, which evidently were worn then by Dutch babies. *Voor-schooten*, which were white bibs; *neerstucken*, which were tuckers, also were worn by little children. Some little Hans of Pieter had given to him by the deacons a fine little scarlet *aperock*, or monkey-jacket; and other children were furnished linen *cosynties*, or night-caps with capes. Yellow stockings were sold at the same time for children, and a gay little yellow turkey-legged Dutchman in a scarlet monkey-jacket and fat little breeches must have been a jolly sight.

CHAPTER X

HOLIDAYS

THE most important holidays of the early years of the colony were, apparently, New Year's Day and May Day, for we find them named through frequent legislation about rioting on these days, repairing of damages, etc. It has been said that New Yorkers owe to the Dutch an everlasting gratitude for our high-stoop houses and the delights of over two centuries of New Year's calling. The latter custom lived long and happily in our midst, died a lingering and lamented death, is still much honored in our memory, and its extinction deeply deplored and unwillingly accepted.

The observance of New Year's Day was, without doubt, followed by both Dutch and English from the earliest settlement. We know that Governor Stuyvesant received New Year's calls, and we also know that he

COLONIAL DAYS

prohibited excessive "drunken drinking," unnecessary firing of guns, and all disorderly behavior on that day. The reign of the English did not abolish New Year's visits; and we find Charles Wolley, an English chaplain, writing in his journal in New York in 1701, of the addition of the English custom of exchange of gifts: —

"The English in New York observed one anniversary custom and that without superstition, I mean the strenarum commercium, as Suetonius calls them, a neighborly commerce of presents every New Year's Day. Some would send me a sugar-loaf, some a pair of gloves, some a bottle or two of wine."

A further celebration of the day by men in New York was by going in parties to Beekman's Swamp to shoot at turkeys.

New Year's calling was a new fashion to General Washington when he came to New York to live for a short time, but he adopted it with approval; and his New Year's Receptions were imposing functions.

For a long time the New Year was ushered in, in country towns, with great noise as well as rejoicing. All through the day groups of men would go from house to house firing salutes, and gathering gradually into large parties by recruits from each house until the end of the day was spent in firing at a mark. The Legislature in March, 1773, attempted to stop the gun-firing, asserting that "great damages are frequently done on the eve of the last day of December and on the first and second days of January by persons going from house to house with guns and other firearms." In 1785 a similar enactment was passed by the State Legislature.

In the palmiest days of New Year's calling, New York City appeared one great family reunion. Every wheeled vehicle in the town seemed to be loaded with visitors going from house to house. Great four and six horse stages packed with hilarious mobs of men went to the house of every acquaintance of every one in the stage. Target companies had processions; political bodies called on families whose head was well known in political life. The newspaper-carriers brought out addresses yards long with rhymes: —

> "The day devoted is to mirth,
> And now around the social hearth
> Friendship unlocks her genial springs,
> And Harmony her lyre now strings.

COLONIAL DAYS

> While plenty spreads her copious hoard,
> And piles and crowns the festive board,"

etc., etc., for hundreds of lines.

The "copious hoard" of substantial food, with decanters of wine, bowls of milk punch, and pitchers of egg-nog, no longer "crown the festive board" on New Year's Day; but we still have New Year's Cakes, though not delivered by singing bakers' 'prentices as of yore.

May Day was observed in similar fashion, — by firing of guns, gay visiting, and also by the rearing of maypoles.

A very early mention of a maypole is in June, 1645, when one William Garritse had "sung a libellous song" against Rev. Francis Doughty, the preacher at Flushing, Long Island, and was sentenced in punishment therefor to be tied to the maypole, which in June was still standing. Stuyvesant again forbade "drunken drinking," and firing of guns and planting of maypoles, as productive of bad practices. I don't know whether the delight of my childhood, and of generations of children in Old and New England up to this present May Day on which I am now writing, — the hanging of May baskets, — ever made happy children in New York.

IN OLD NEW YORK

There was some observance in New York of Shrovetide as a holiday-time. As early as 1657 we find the sober Beverwyck burghers deliberating on "some improprieties committed at the house of Albert de Timmerman on Shrovetide last." As was the inevitable custom followed by the extremely uninventive brain of the seventeenth and eighteenth century rioter, were he Dutch or English, these "improprieties" took the form of the men's parading in women's clothes; Pieter Semiensen was one of the masqueraders. Two years later the magistrates were again investigating the "unseemly and scandalous" celebration of Shrovetide; and as ever before, the youth of early Albany donned women's clothes and "marched as mountebanks," as the record says, just as they did in Philadelphia and Baltimore and even in sober Boston. We find also for sale in Beverwyck at this time, noisy Shrovetide toys — *rommelerytiens*, little "rumbling-pots," which the youth and children doubtless keenly enjoyed.

At an early date Shrovetide observances, such as "pulling the goose," were prohibited by Governor Stuyvesant in New York. A mild protest on the part of some of the burgomasters against this order of the Governor brought forth one of Stuyvesant's characteristically choleric edicts in answer, in which he speaks of having "interdicted and forbidden certain farmers' servants to ride the goose at the feast of Backus and Shrovetide ... because it is altogether unprofitable, unnecessary, and criminal for subjects and neighbors to celebrate such pagan and popish feasts and to practise such customs, notwithstanding the same may in some places of Fatherland be tolerated and looked at through the fingers." Domine Blom, of Kingston or Wyltwyck, joined in the governor's dislike of the game. But there were some of the magistrates who liked very well to "pull the goose" themselves, so it is said. It was a cruel amusement. The thoroughly greased goose was hung between two poles, and the effort of the sport was to catch, snatch away, and hold fast the poor creature while passing at great speed. In Albany in 1677 all "Shrovetide misdemeanors were prohibited, viz.: riding at a goose, cat, hare, and ale." The fine was twenty-five guilders in sea-want. What the cat, hare, and ale part of the sport was, I do not know.

IN OLD NEW YORK

In New York by the middle of the eighteenth century Shrove Tuesday was firmly assigned to cocking-mains. The De Lanceys were patrons of this choice old English sport. Cock-gaffs of silver and steel were freely offered for sale in New York and Maryland newspapers, and on Shrove Tuesday in 1770 Jacob Hiltzeheimer attended a famous cock-fight on the Germantown road. We cannot blame honest New Yorkers if they did not rise above such rude sports, when cock-fighting and cock-throwing and cock-squoiling and cock-steling obtained everywhere in Old England at Shrovetide; when school-boys had cock-fights in their school-rooms; and in earlier days good and learned old Roger Ascham ruined himself by betting on cock-fights, and Sir Thomas More boasted proudly of his skill in "casting a cock-stele."

Mr. Gabriel Furman, writing in 1846, told of an extraordinary observance of Saint Valentine's Day by the Dutch — one I think unknown in folk-lore — which obtained on Long Island among the early settlers. It was called *Vrouwen dagh*, or Women's day, and was thus celebrated: Every young girl sallied forth in the morning armed with a heavy cord with knotted end. She gave to every young man whom she met several smart lashes with the knotted cord. Perhaps these were "love-taps," and were given with no intent of stinging. Judge Egbert Benson wrote, in 1816, that in New York this custom dwindled to a similar Valentine observance by New York children, when the girls chased the boys with many blows. In one school the boys asked for a *Mannen dagh* in which to repay the girls' stinging lashes. I hazard a " wide solution," as Sir Thomas Browne says, that this custom is a commemorative survival of an event in the life of Saint Valentine, one of the two traditions which are all we know of his life, that about the year 270 he was "first beaten with heavy clubs and then beheaded."

The English brought a political holiday to New York. In the code of laws given to the province in 1665, and known as " The Duke's Laws," each minister throughout the province was ordered to preach a sermon on November 5, to commemorate the English deliverance from Guy Fawkes and the Gunpowder Plot in 1605.

From an early entry in the " New York Gazette" of November 7, 1737, we learn how it was celebrated that year, and find that illuminations, as in England, formed part of the day's remembrance. Bonfires, fantastic processions, and "burning a Guy" formed, in fact, the chief English modes of celebration.

"Saturday last, being the fifth of November, it was observed here in Memory of that horrid and Treasonable Popish Gun-Powder Plot to blow up and destroy King, Lords and Commons, and the Gentlemen of his Majesty's Council; the Assembly and Corporation and other the principal Gentlemen and Merchants of this City waited upon his Honor the Lieutenant-Governor at Fort George, where the Royal Healths were drunk, as usual, under the discharge of the Cannon, and at the Night the city was illuminated."

All through the English provinces bonfires were burned, effigies were carried in procession, mummers and masqueraders thronged the streets and invaded the houses singing Pope Day rhymes, and volleys of guns were fired. In some New England towns the boys still have bonfires on November 5th.

In the year 1765 the growing feeling with regard to the Stamp Act chancing to come to a climax in the late autumn, produced in New York a very riotous observance of Pope's Day. The demonstrations really began on November 1st, which was termed "The Last Day of Liberty." In the evening a mob gathered, "designing to execute some foolish ceremony of burying Liberty," but it dispersed with noise and a few broken windows. The next night a formidable mob gathered, "carrying candles and torches in their hands, and now and then firing a pistol at the Effigy which was carried in a Chair." Then the effigy was set in the Governor's chariot, which was taken out of the Fort. They made a gallows and hung on it an effigy of the Governor and one of the Devil, and carried it to the Fort, over which insult soldiers and officers were wonderfully patient. Finally, gallows, chariot and effigies were all burnt in the Bowling Green. The mob then ransacked Major James's house, eating, drinking, destroying, till £1500 of damage was done. The next day it was announced that the delivery and destruction of the stamps would be demanded. In the evening the mob started out again, with candles and a barber's block dressed in rags. The rioters finally dispersed at the entreaties of many good citizens, — among them Robert R. Livingstone, who wrote the letter from which this account is taken. In 1774, November 5th was still a legal holiday.

There still exists in New York a feeble and divided survival of the processions and bonfires of Guy Fawkes Day. The police-prohibited bonfires of barrels on election night, and the bedraggled parade of begging boys on Thanksgiving Day are our reminders to-day of this old English holiday.

There was one old-time holiday beloved of New Yorkers whose name is now almost forgotten, — Pinkster Day. This name was derived from the Dutch word for Pentecost, and must have been used at a very early date; for in a Dutch book of sermons, written by Adrian Fischer, and printed in 1667, the title of one sermon reads: *Het Eersts Tractact; Van de Uystortnge des Yeyligen Geests over de Apostelen op ben Pinckster Dagh*, — a sermon upon the story of the Descent of the Holy Ghost on the Apostles on Pinkster Day.

The Jewish feast of Pentecost was observed on the fiftieth day after the celebration of the Passover, and is the same as the Christian holy-day Whitsunday, which is connected with its Jewish predecessor historically (as is so beautifully told in the second chapter of Acts), and intrinsically through its religious signification. The week following Whitsunday has been observed with great honor and rejoicing in many lands, but in none more curiously, more riotously, than in old New York, and to some extent in Pennsylvania and Maryland; and, more strangely still, that observance was chiefly by an alien, a heathen race, — the negroes. It was one of our few distinctively American folk-customs, and its story has been told by many writers of that day, and should not now be forgotten. Nowhere was it a more glorious festival than at Albany, among the sheltered, the cherished slave population in that town and its vicinity. The celebration was held on Capitol Hill, then universally known as Pinkster Hill. Munsell gives this account of the day: —

"Pinkster was a great day, a gala day, or rather week, for they used to keep it up a week among the darkies. The dances were the original Congo dances as danced in their native Africa. They had a chief, — Old King Charley. The old settlers said Charley was a prince in his own country, and was supposed to have been one hundred and twenty-five years old at the time of his death. On these festivals old Charley was dressed in a strange and fantastical costume; he was nearly barelegged, wore a red military coat trimmed profusely with variegated ribbons, and a small black hat with a pompon stuck on one side. The dances and antics of the darkies must have afforded great amusement for the ancient burghers. As a general thing, the music consisted of a sort of drum, or instrument constructed out of a box with sheepskin heads, upon which old Charley did most of the beating, accompanied by singing some queer African air. Charley generally led off the dance, when the Sambos and Phillises, juvenile and antiquated, would put in the double-shuffle heel-and-toe breakdown. These festivals seldom failed to attract large crowds from the city, as well as from the rural districts."

Dr. Eights, of Albany, wrote still further reminiscences of the day. He said that, strangely enough, though all the booths and sports opened on Monday, white curiosity-seekers were, on that first day, the chief visitors to Pinkster Hill. On Tuesday the blacks all appeared, and the consumption of gingerbread, cider, and applejack began.

COLONIAL DAYS

Adam Blake, a truly elegant creature, the body-servant of the old patroon Van Rensselaer, was master of the ceremonies. Charley, the King, was a "Guinea man" from Angola, — and I have noted the fact that nearly all African-born negroes who became leaders in this country, or men of marked note in any way, have been Guinea men. He wore portions of the costume of a British general, and had the power of an autocrat, — his will was law. Dr. Eights says the Pinkster musical instruments were eel-pots covered with dressed sheepskin, on which the negroes pounded with their bare hands, as do all savage nations on their tom-toms. Their song had an African refrain, "Hi-a-bomba-bomba-bomba." Other authorities state that the dance was called the "Toto Dance," and partook so largely of savage license that at last the white visitors shunned being present during its performance.

These Pinkster holidays became such bacchanalian revels in other ways that in 1811 the Common Council of Albany prohibited the erection of booths and all dancing, gaming, and drinking at that time; and when the negroes could not dance nor drink, it was but a sorry holiday, and quickly fell into desuetude.

Executions were held on Pinkster Hill, and other public punishments took place there.

In the realm of fiction we find evidence of the glories of Pinkster Day in New York. Cooper, in his "Satanstoe," tells of its observance in New York City. He calls it the saturnalia of the blacks, and says that they met on what we now know as City Hall Park, and that the negroes came for thirty or forty miles around to join in the festivities.

On Long Island Pinkster Day was widely observed. The blacks went, on the week previous to the celebration, to Brooklyn and New York to sell sassafras and swingling-tow, to earn their scanty spending-money for Pinkster. They were everywhere freely given their time for rioting, and domestic labor was performed by the masters and mistresses; but they had to provide their own spending-money for gingerbread and rum. They gathered around the old market in Brooklyn near the ferry, dancing for eels, blowing fish-horns, eating and drinking.

COLONIAL DAYS

The following morning the judge's office was full of sorry blacks, hauled up for "disorderly conduct."

On Long Island the Dutch residents also made the day a festival, "going to pinkster fields for pinkster frolics," exchanging visits, and drinking schnapps, and eating "soft-wafels" together. About twelve years ago, while driving through Flatlands and New Lots one beautiful day in May, I met a group of young men driving from door to door of the farm-houses, in wagons gayly dressed with branches of dogwood blossoms, and entering each house for a short visit. I asked whether a wedding or a festival were being held in the town, and was answered that it was an old Dutch custom to make visits that week. I tried to learn whence this observance came, but no one knew its reason for being, or what holiday was observed. Poor Pinkster! still vaguely honored as a shadow, a ghost of the past, but with your very name forgotten, even among the children of those who gave to you in this land a name and happy celebration!

Various wild flowers were known as Pinkster flowers. The beautiful azalea that once

IN OLD NEW YORK

bloomed — indeed does still bloom — so plentifully throughout New York in May, was universally known as "pinkster flower" or "pinkster bloom," and along the banks of the Hudson till our own day was called "pinkster blummachee." The traveller Kalm noted it in 1740, and called it by that name. Mrs. Vanderbilt calls it "pinkster bloomitze." I was somewhat surprised to hear a Rhode Island farmer, in the summer of 1893, ask me whether he should not pick me "some pinkster blossoms," pointing at the same time to the beautiful swamp pink that flushed with rosy glow the tangles of vines and bushes on the edge of the Narragansett woods. It is interesting to know that by many authorities the name "pink," of our common garden flower, is held to be derived from the Dutch *Pinkster*, German *Pfingsten*, and owes its name, not to its pink color, but to the season of its blooming. In other localities in New York and New Jersey the blue flag or iris was known as "pinkster bloom."

Throughout New England the black residents, free and in bondage, held high holiday one day in May, or in some localities during the first week in June; but the day of revelry was everywhere called "Nigger 'Lection." In Puritandom the observance of Whitsunday was believed to have "superstition writ on its forehead;" but Election Day was a popular and properly Puritanical May holiday; therefore the negro holiday took a similar name, and the "Black Governor" was elected on the week following the election of the white Governor, usually on Saturday.

There was some celebration of days of thanksgiving in New Netherland as in Holland; they were known by a peculiar double name, fast-prayer and thank-day. These days did not develop among the Dutch in the new world into the position of importance they held among English colonists. In 1644 the first public Thanksgiving Day whose record has come down to us was proclaimed in gratitude for the safe return of the Dutch warriors after a battle with the Connecticut Indians on Strickland's Plains near Stamford. A second Thanksgiving service was announced for the 6th of September, 1645, whereon God was to be "specially thanked, praised, and blessed for suffering" the long-wished-for peace with the Indians. This service was held on Wednesday, which was usually the chosen day of the week. In 1654, at a Thanksgiving ordered on account of the peace established between England and the Netherlands, services were to be held in the morning; the citizens were to be permitted "to indulge in all moderate festivities and rejoicings as the event recommends and their Situation Shall permit." That these festivities were not always decorous is shown by the fining and punishment of some young lads for drunkenness on one Thanksgiving Day.

Various were the causes of the commemorative services: peace between Spain and the Fatherland; the prosperity of the province, its peace, increased people, and trade; a harvest of self-sown grain (the fields having been deserted for fear of Indians). In 1664 Domine Brown, of Wyltwyck, asked for an established annual Thanksgiving; but there are no records to show that this desire was carried out, though from 1690 to 1710 they were held almost every year.

CHAPTER XI

AMUSEMENTS AND SPORTS

DANIEL DENTON, one of the original settlers of Jamaica, Long Island, wrote "A briefe Description of New York" in 1670. When he speaks of the "fruits natural to the island" of Long Island, he ends his account thus: —

"Such abundance of strawberries is in June that the fields and woods are dyed red; which the country people perceiving, instantly arm themselves with bottles of wine, cream, and sugar, and instead of a coat of Mail every one takes a Female upon his Horse behind him, and so rushing violently into the fields, never leave till they have disrobed them of their red colors and turned them into the old habit."

"Rushing violently into the fields" seems to have been the normal condition of all the colonists as soon as the tardy American "spring came slowly up the way." On every hand they turned eagerly to open-air outings. Houses chafed them; gipsy-like were they in their love of fresh air and the country wilds.

In New York were the bouweries close at hand; and Nutten Island (now Governor's Island), " by ye making of a garden and planting severall walks of fruit trees in it," made a pretty outing-spot. Mrs. Grant wrote at length of the Albany youth and their love of out-of-door excursions: —

"In spring, eight or ten of the young people of one company, or related to each other, young men and maidens, would set out together in a canoe on a kind of rural excursion, of which amusement was the object. Yet so fixed were their habits of industry that they never failed to carry their work-baskets with them, not as a form, but as an ingredient necessarily mixed with their pleasures. They had no attendants, and steered a devious course of four, five, or perhaps more miles, till they arrived at some of the beautiful islands with which this fine river abounded, or at some sequestered spot on its banks, where delicious wild fruits, or particular conveniences for fishing, afforded some attraction. There they generally arrived by nine or ten o'clock, having set out in the cool and early hour of sunrise. . . . A basket with tea, sugar, and the other usual provisions for breakfast, with the apparatus for cooking it; a little rum and fruit for making cool weak punch, the usual beverage in the middle of the day, and now and then some cold pastry, was the sole provision; for the great affair was to depend on the sole exertions of the boys in procuring fish, wild ducks, &c., for their dinner. They were all, like Indians, ready and dexterous with the axe, gun, &c. Whenever they arrived at their destination, they sought out a dry and beautiful spot opposite to the river, and in an instant with their axes cleared so much superfluous shade or shrubbery as left a semicircular opening, above which they bent and twined the boughs, so as to form a pleasant bower, while the girls gathered dried branches, to which one of the youths soon set fire with gunpowder, and the breakfast, a very regular and cheerful one, occupied an hour or two. The young men then set out to fish, or perhaps to shoot birds, and the maidens sat busily down to their work. After the sultry hours had been thus employed, the boys brought their tribute from the river or the wood, and found a rural meal prepared by their fair companions, among whom were generally their sisters and the chosen of their hearts. After dinner they all set out together to gather wild strawberries, or whatever other fruit was in season; for it was accounted a reflection to come home empty-handed. When wearied of this amusement, they either drank tea in their bower, or, returning, landed at some friend's on the way, to partake of that refreshment."

Suburban taverns were much resorted to at a little later date by all town-folk, and "ladies and gentlemen were entertained in the genteelest manner." New Yorkers specially liked the fish-dinners furnished at an inn perched on Brooklyn Heights; and twice a week they could drive to a turtle-feast at a beloved retreat on the East River, always taking much care to return over the Kissing Bridge, where, says with approval a reverend gentleman, a traveller of ante-Revolutionary days, "it is part of the etiquette to salute the lady who has put herself under your protection." More idyllic still was the rowing across the river to Brooklyn, to the noble tulip-tree near the ferry, with its great spreading shadowy branches, so cool in summer suns, and glorious with tropical blooms, and hospitable with a vast shining hollow trunk which would hold six or eight happy summer revellers within the sheltering walls. Would I could sing The Tulip-Tree as Cowper did The Sofa; with its happy summer groups, its beauty, its pathetic end, and the simple joys it sheltered, — as extinct as the species to which the tree itself belongs!

Occasional glimpses of pretty country hospitality in country homes are afforded through old-time letters. One of the Rutherfurd letters reads: —

"We were very elegantly entertained at the Clarks', and everything of their own production. By way of amusement after dinner we all went into the garden to pick roses. We gathered a large basket full, and prepared them for distilling. As I had never seen Rose-water made, Mrs. Clark got her still and set it going, and made several bottles while we were there. They were extremely civil, and begged us whenever we rode that way in the evening to stop and take a syllabub with them."

This certainly presents a very dainty scene; the sweet June rose-garden, the delicate housewifery, the drinking of syllabubs make it seem more French than plain New York Dutch in tone and color.

The Dutch were no haters of games as were the Puritans; games were known and played even in the time of the first settlers. Steven Janse had a *tick-tack bort* at Fort Orange. Tick-tack was a complicated kind of backgammon, played with both men and pegs. "The Compleat Gamester" says tick-tack is so called from touch and take, for if you touch a man you must play him though to your loss. "Tick-tacking" was prohibited during time of divine service in New Amsterdam in 1656. Another Dutch tapster had a trock-table, which Florio says was "a kind of game used in England with casting little bowles at a boord with thirteen holes in it." A trock-table was a table much like a pool table, on which an ivory ball was struck under a wire wicket by a cue. Trock was also played on the grass, — a seventeenth-century modification of croquet. Of bowling we hear plenty of talk; it was universally played, from clergy down to negro slaves, and a famous street in New York, the Bowling Green, perpetuates its popularity. The English brought card-playing and gaming, to which the Dutch never abandoned themselves.

By the middle of the eighteenth century we find more amusements and a gayer life. The first regularly banded company of comedians which played in New York strayed thence from Philadelphia in March, 1750, where they had been bound over to good behavior, and where their departure had given much joy to a disgusted Quaker community. It was called Murray and Kean's company, and sprung up in Philadelphia like a toadstool in a night, from whence or how no one knows. The comedians announced their "sitting down" in New York for the season. They opened with King Richard III., "written by Shakespeare and improved by Colley Cibber." They also played "The Beau in the Sudds," "The Spanish Fryer," "The Orphan," "The Beau's Stratagem," "The Constant Couple," "The Lying Valet," "The Twin Rivals," "Colin and Phœbe," "Love for Love," "The Stagecoach," "The Recruiting Officer," "Cato," "Amphitryon," "Sir Harry Wildair," "George Barnwell," "Bold Stroke for a Wife," "Beggar's Opera," "The Mock Doctor," "The Devil to Pay," "The Fair Penitent," "The Virgin Unmasked," "Miss in her Teens," and a variety of pantomimes and farces. This was really a very good series of bills, but the actors were a sorry lot. One was a redemptioner, Mrs. Davis, and she had a benefit to help to buy her freedom; another desired a benefit, as he was "just out of prison." They were in town ten months, and seem to have been on very friendly terms with the public, borrowing single copies of plays to study from, having constant benefits, ending with one for Mr. Kean, in which one Mrs. Taylor was "out so much in her part" that she had to be apologized for afterwards in the newspapers. She had a benefit shortly after, at which, naturally and properly, there "was n't much company." Miss George at her benefit had bad weather and other disappointments, and tried it over again. At last Mr. Kean, "by the advice of several Gentlemen having resolv'd to quit the stage and follow his Employment of writing and hopes for Encouragement," sold his half of "his cloaths" and the stage effects for a benefit, at which if the house had been full to overflowing the whole receipts would not have been more than two hundred and fifty dollars. John Tremain also "declined the stage" and went to cabinet-making, — "plain and scallopt tea-tables, etc.,"—which was very sensible, since tea was more desired than the drama. A new company sprung up, but "mett with small encouragement," though the company " assured the Publick they are

COLONIAL DAYS

Perfect and hope to Perform to Satisfaction." Perhaps the expression "the Part of Lavinia will be *Attempted* by Mrs. Tremain" was a wise one. All this was at a time when a good theatrical company could easily have been obtained in England, where the art of the actor was at a high standard.

We gain a notion of some rather trying manners at these theatres. The English custom of gentlemen's crowding on the stage increased to such an extent, and proved so deleterious to any good representation of the play, that the manager advertised in "Gaines' Mercury," in 1762, that no spectators would be permitted to stand or sit on the stage during the performance. And also a reproof was printed to "the person so very rude as to throw Eggs from the Gallery upon the stage, to the injury of Cloaths."

For some years a Mr. Bonnin, a New York fishmonger, entertained his fellow-citizens and those of neighboring towns with various scientific exhibits, lectures, camera obscuras, "prospects" and "perspectives," curious animals, "Philosophical-Optical machines" and wax-works, and manifold other performances, which he ingeniously altered and renamed.

He was a splendid advertiser. The newspapers of the times contain many of his attempts to catch the public attention. I give two as an example: —

"We hear that Mr. Bonnin is so crouded with company to view his Perspectives, that he can scarce get even so much time as to eat, drink or say his Prayers, from the time he gets out of bed till He repairs to it again: and it is the Opinion of some able Physicians that if he makes rich, it must be at the Expense of the Health of his Body, and of some Learned Divines it must be at the Expense of the Welfare of His Soul."

"The common topics of discourse here since the coming of Mr. Bonnin are entirely changed. Instead of the common chat nothing is scarce mentioned now but the most entertaining parts of Europe which are represented so lively in Mr. Bonnin's curious Prospects."

Mr. Bonnin is now but a shadow of the past, vanished like his puppets into nowhere; in his own far "perspective" of a century and a half, he seems to me amusing; at any rate, he was all that New Yorkers had many times to amuse them; and I think he must have been a jolly lecturer, when he was such a jolly advertiser.

COLONIAL DAYS

Also in evidence before the public was one Pachebell, a musician. The following is one of his advertisements in the year 1734: —

"On Wednesday the 21st of January instant there will be a Consort of music, vocal and instrumental for the benefit of Mr. Pachebell, the harpsicord parts performed by himself. The songs, violins and German flutes by private hands. The Consort will begin precisely at six o'clock in the house of Robert Todd vintner. Tickets to be had at the Coffee House at 4 shillings."

Amateurs often performed for his benefit, and even portions of oratorios were "attempted." His "consorts" were said to be ravishing, and inspired the listeners to rhapsodic poesy, which is more than can be said of many concerts nowadays. Those who know the "thin metallic thrills" of a harpsichord — an instrument with no resonance, mellowness, or singing quality — can reflect upon the susceptibility of our ancestors, who could melt into sentiment and rhyme over those wiry vibrations.

The favorite winter amusement in New York, as in Philadelphia, was riding in sleighs, a fashion which the Dutch brought from Holland. The English colonists in New England were slower to adopt sleighs for carriages, and never in early days found sleighing a sport. The bitter New England weather did not attract sleighers.

Madam Knights, a Boston visitor to New York, wrote in 1704: —

"Their diversion in winter is riding in sleighs about three miles out of town, where they have houses of entertainment at a place called the Bowery; and some go to friends' houses, who handsomely treat them. I believe we mett fifty or sixty sleighs one day; they fly with great swiftness, and some are so furious that they turn out for none except a loaded cart."

An English parson, one Burnaby, visiting New York in 1759, wrote of their delightful sleighing-parties; and Mrs. Anne Grant thus adds her testimony of similar pleasures in Albany: —

"In winter the river, frozen to a great depth, formed the principal road through the country, and was the scene of all those amusements of skating and sledge races, common to the north of Europe. They used in great parties to visit their friends at a distance, and having an excellent and hardy breed of horses, flew from place to place over the snow or ice in these sledges with incredible rapidity, stopping a little while at every house they came to, and always well received whether acquainted with the owners or not. The night never impeded these travellers, for the atmosphere was so pure and serene, and the snow so reflected the moon and star-light, that the nights exceeded the days in beauty."

William Livingstone, when he was twenty-one years old, wrote in 1744 of a "waffle-frolic," which was an amusement then in vogue: —

"We had the wafel-frolic at Miss Walton's talked of before your departure. The feast as usual was preceded by cards, and the company so numerous that they filled two tables; after a few games, a magnificent supper appeared in grand order and decorum, but for my own part I was not a little grieved that so luxurious a feast should come under the name of a wafel-frolic, because if this be the case I must expect but a few wafel-frolics for the future; the frolic was closed up with *ten sunburnt virgins lately come from Columbus's Newfoundland*, besides a play of my own invention which I have not room enough to describe at present. However, kissing constitutes a great part of its entertainment."

Kissing seemed to constitute a great part of the entertainment at evening parties everywhere at that time.

IN OLD NEW YORK

As soon as the English obtained control of New York, they established English sports and pastimes, among them fox-hunting. Long Island afforded good sport. During the autumn three days' hunting was permitted at Flatbush; in other towns the chase was stolen fun. A woman-satirist, with a spirited pen, had her fling in rhyme at fox-hunting. Here are a few of her lines: —

> "A fox is killed by twenty men,
> That fox perhaps had killed a hen.
> A gallant art no doubt is here,
> All wicked foxes ought to fear,
> When twenty dogs and twenty men
> Can kill a fox that killed a hen."

Fox-hunting was never very congenial, apparently, to those of Dutch descent and Dutch characteristics; nor was cock-fighting, the prevalence of which I have noted in the preceding chapter. Occasionally we hear of the cruel sport of bull-baiting, though not till the latter half of the eighteenth century. In 1763 the keeper of the DeLancey Arms on the Bowery Lane gave a bull-baiting. Brooklyn was specially favored in that respect during the Revolution, when the British officers took charge of and enjoyed the barbarism,

COLONIAL DAYS

and Landlord Loosely of the King's Head Tavern helped in the arrangements and advertising. Good active bulls and strong dogs were in much demand. The newspapers of the times contain many advertisements of the sport. One in poor rhyme begins: —

> "This notice gives to all who covet
> Baiting the bull and dearly love it." etc.

I frequently recall, as I pass through a quiet street near my home, that in the year 1774 a bull-baiting was held there every afternoon for many months, and I resolutely demolish that hollow idol — the good old times — and rejoice in humane to-day.

As early as 1665 Governor Nicholls announced that a horse-race would take place at Hempstead, "not so much for the divertissement of youth as for encouraging the bettering of the breed of horses which through great neglect has been impaired." In 1669 Governor Lovelace gave orders that a race should be run in May each year, and that subscriptions should be sent to Captain Salisbury, "of all such as are disposed to run for a crown in silver or the value thereof in wheat." This first course was a naturally level plain called Salisbury Plains, and was so named after this very Captain Silvester Salisbury, Commander of Royal Troops in the province, and an enthusiastic sportsman. Its location was near the present Hyde Park station of Long Island.

Daniel Denton, one of the early settlers of Jamaica, Long Island, wrote in 1670 thus: —

"Towards the middle of Long Island lieth a plain sixteen miles long and four broad, upon which plain grows very fine grass that makes exceeding good hay; where you shall find neither stick nor stone to hinder the horse-heels, or endanger them in their races, and once a year the best horses in the island are brought hither to try their Swiftness and the swiftest rewarded with a silver Cup, two being Annually procured for the Purpose."

The "fine grass" was what was known as secretary grass, and, curiously enough, this great plain was abandoned to this growth of secretary grass for more than a century after the settlement and cultivation of surrounding farms; this was through a notion that the soil was too porous to be worth ploughing. Even a clergyman sent out by the Society for

COLONIAL DAYS

the Propagation of the Gospel in Foreign Parts testified to the beauty of Salisbury Plain, calling it "an even delightsome plain, most sweet and pleasant." Delightsome it certainly proved to lovers of horse-racing.

On February 24, 1721, a race was held on this plain which attracted much attention. The winning horse was owned by Samuel Bayard. The race was given by "the inhabitants of Queens County on Nassau Island." The name of the course had by this time been changed to Newmarket. In 1764 a new course was laid out; and in 1804 the racing moved to a field east of the Old Court House, and in 1821 it was transferred to the Union Course on the western border of Jamaica. The story of this course is familiar to sportsmen.

Frequent newspaper notices call attention to the races held at this Hempstead Newmarket. From the "New York Postboy" of June 4, 1750, I quote: —

"On Friday last there was a great horse race on Hempstead Plains which engaged the attention of so many of the city of New York that upwards of seventy chairs and chaises were carried over Brooklyn Ferry the day before, besides a far greater number of horses. The number of horses on the plains exceeded, it is thought, one thousand."

In 1764 we find the Macaroni Club offering prizes of £100 and £50. At those races Mr. James De Lancey's bay horse Lath won. On September 28, 1769, the same horse Lath won a £100 race in Philadelphia.

In October, 1770, Jacob Hiltzheimer, a well-known lover and breeder of horses in Philadelphia, went to the races on Hempstead Plains, and lodged at a "public house" in Jamaica, with various other gentlemen,— lovers of races. Two purses of £50 were given, but Mr. Hiltzheimer's chestnut horse Regulus did not win.

A London racing-book of 1776 says of this Hempstead course: —

"These plains were celebrated for their races throughout all the Colonies and even in England. They were held twice a year for a silver cup, to which the gentry of New England and New York resorted."

Another famous race-course of colonial days was the one-mile course around Beaver Pond in Jamaica. This was laid out before

COLONIAL DAYS

the year 1757, for on June 13 of that year a subscription plate was won by Lewis Morris, Jr., with his horse American Childers. Another course was at Newtown in 1758, and another at New Lots in 1778.

I find frequent allusions in the colonial press to the Beaver Pond course. The "New York Mercury" of 1763 tells of a "Free Masons' Purse" — for best two in three heats, each heat three times round Beaver Pond — freemasons were to be "inspectors" of this race.

At the time of the possession of Brooklyn and western Long Island by the British during the Revolutionary War, there constantly went on a succession of sporting events of all kinds under the direction of the English officers and a notorious tavern-keeper Loosely, already named, who seemed to devote every energy to the amusement of the English invaders. An advertisement in "Rivington's Gazette" November 4, 1780, reads thus : —

"By Permission Three Days' Sport on Ascot Heath formerly Flatlands Plain on Monday. 1. The Noblemen's and Gentlemen's Purse of £60 free for any horse except Mr. Wortman's and Mr. Allen's Dulcimore who won the plate at Beaver Pond last season. 2. A Saddle, bridle, and whip, worth £15 for ponies not exceeding 13½ hands. Tuesday. 1. Ladies' Subscription Purse of £50. 2. To be run for by women, a Holland smock and Chintz Gown full-trimmed; to run the two in three quarter-miles; first to have the smock and gown of four guineas value; second, a guinea; third half a guinea. Wednesday. Country Subscription Purse of £50. No person will erect a booth or sell liquor without subscribing 2 guineas to expenses of races. Gentlemen fond of fox-hunting will meet at Loosely's Kings Head Tavern at day break during the races. God Save the King played every hour."

It will be seen by this advertisement that the rough and rollicking ways of English holidays were introduced in this woman's-race. The women who ran those quarter-miles must have been some camp-followers, for I am sure no honest Long Island country-girls would have taken part. At other races on this freshly named "Ascot Heath" hurling-matches and bull-baitings and lotteries added their zest, and on April 27, 1782, there was a three hundred guineas sweep-stakes race. These races were held at short intervals until October, 1783, when English sports and English cruelties no longer held sway on Long Island.

At these races, given under martial rule, some rather crooked proceedings were taken to recruit the field and keep up the interest; and good horses for many miles around were watched carefully by their owners; and when a gentleman attending the races viewed with surprised and indignant recognition his own horse which had been stolen from him, he promptly applied for restitution to Mr. Cornell, of Brooklyn, who had entered the horse; and when the race was finished, the horse was returned to its rightful owner.

Other localities developed race-courses. "At Captain Tim Cornell's Poles, on Hempstead Plains," Eclipse and Sturdy Beggar ran for "Fifty Joes" on March 14, 1781. In 1783 Eclipse and Young Slow and Easy ran for a purse of two hundred guineas. At Far Rockaway, in 1786, Jacob Hicks, "from a wish to gratify sportsmen," laid out a mile course and offered prizes where no "trussing, jostling, or foul play were countenanced; if detected, the rider will be pronounced distanced."

On Manhattan Island were several other

race-courses. In 1742, a race was run on the Church Farm, just a stone's throw northwest of where the Astor House now stands. I have seen many notices of races on this Church Farm which was the valuable Trinity Church property. In October, 1726, a Subscription Plate of twenty pounds was run for "on the Course at New York." The horses were entered with Francis Child on Fresh Water Hill. Entrance fee was half a pistole. Admission to the public, sixpence each. In the 1750 October runs, Mr. Lewis Morris, Jr.'s horse won on the Church Farm course. The chief racing stables in the province of New York were those of Mr. Morris and of Mr. James De Lancey. The former won a reputation with American Childers; the latter with his imported horse Lath. The De Lancey stables were the most costly ones in the north; their colors were seen on every course for ten years previous to the Revolution, and they were patrons of all English sports. A famous horse of James De Lancey's was True Briton. It is told of this horse that Oliver De Lancey would jump him back and forth from a standstill over a five-barred gate. There was a course at

Greenwich Village on the estate of Sir Peter Warren, and one at Harlem, another at Newburgh.

Many advertisements of other races with names of horses and owners might be added to this list; but I think I have given a sufficient number to disprove the vague assertions of Frank Forester and other writers of the history of the horse in America, that little attention was paid to horse-raising in the northern provinces, and that there were a few races on Long Island previous to the Revolution, but it is not known whether taking place regularly, or for given prizes. There was no racing-calendar in America till 1829, but there are other ways of learning of races.

IN OLD NEW YORK

CHAPTER XII

CRIMES AND PUNISHMENTS

THE court records of any period in our American history are an unfailing source of profit and delight to the historian. In the town or state whose colonial records still exist there can ever be drawn a picture not only of the crimes and punishments, but of the manners, occupations, and ways of our ancestors and a knowledge can be gained of the social ethics, the morality, the modes of thought, the intelligence of dead-and-gone citizens. We learn that they had daily hopes and plans and interests and harassments just such as our own, as well as vices and wickedness.

In spite of Chancellor Kent's assertion of their dulness and lack of interest, the court records of Dutch colonial times are not to me dull reading: quaint humor and curious terms abound; the criminal records always

COLONIAL DAYS

are interesting; even the old *reken-boeks* (the account-books) are of value. These first sources give an unbiassed and well-outlined picture, sometimes a surprising and almost irreconcilable one; for instance, I had always a fixed notion that the early women-colonists of Dutch birth were wholly a quiet, reserved, even timid group; not talkative and never aggressive. It was therefore a great thrust at my established ideas to discover, when poring over an old "Road Book" at the Hall of Records in Brooklyn, containing some entries of an early Court of Sessions, an account of the trial of two dames of Bushwyck, Mistress Jonica Schampf and Widow Rachel Luquer, for assaulting the captain of the Train-Band, Captain Peter Praa, on training-day in October, 1690, while he was at the head of his company. These two vixens most despitefully used him; they beat him, pulled his hair, assaulted and wounded him, and committed "other Ivill Inormities, so that his life was despaired of." And there was no evidence to show that any of his soldiers, or any of the spectators present, interfered to save either Peter's life or his honor. The offence which provoked this assault is not even hinted at, though it may have arisen from the troubled state of public affairs. Captain Praa was a man of influence and dignity in the community, an exiled Huguenot, of remarkable skill in horsemanship and arms. In spite of all this, it appears probable that the sentiment of the community was in sympathy with the two turbulent assaulters and batterers, for they were fined only six shillings and three pounds respectively. They threw themselves on the mercy of the Court, and certainly were treated with mercy.

There are, however, few women-criminals named in the old Dutch and early English records, and these few were not prosecuted for any very great crimes or viciousness; the chief number were brought up for defamation of character and slander, though men-slanderers were more plentiful than women. The close intimacy, the ideal neighborliness of the Dutch communities of New York made the settlers deeply abhor all violations of the law of social kindness. To preserve this state of amity, they believed with Chaucer "the first vertue is to restraine and kepen wel thine tonge."

The magistrates knew how vast a flame might be kindled by a petty spark; and therefore promptly quenched the odious slander in its beginning; petty quarrels were adjusted by arbitration ere they grew to great breaches. As sung the chorus of Batavian women in Van der Vondel's great poem: —

> "If e'er dispute or discord dared intrude,
> 'T was soon by wisdom's voice subdued."

In spite, however, of all wariness and watchfulness and patience, the inevitable fretfulness engendered in petty natures by a narrow and confined life showed in neighborhood disputes and suits for defamation of character, few of them of great seriousness and most of them easily adjusted by the phlegmatic and somewhat dictatorial Dutch magistrates. In a community so given to nicknaming it seems strange to find such extreme touchiness about being called names. Suits for defamation were frequent, through opprobrious name-calling, and on very slight though irritating grounds. It would certainly seem a rather disproportionate amount of trouble to bring a lawsuit simply because you were called a "black pudding," or a *verklickker*, or tale-bearer, or even a "Turk;" though, of course, no one would stand being called a "horned beast" or a "hay thief." Nor was "Thou swine" an offensive term too petty to be passed over in silence. The terrible epithets, *spitter-baard* and "Dutch dough-face," seem to make a climax of opprobriousness; but the word *moff* was worse, for it was the despised term applied in Holland to the Germans, and it led to a quarrel with knives.

I wish to note in passing that though the Dutch called each other these disagreeable and even degrading names, they did not swear at each other. Profanity was seldom punished in New Amsterdam, for practically it did not exist, as was remarked by travellers. Chaplain Wolley told of "the usual oath" of one Dutch colonist, — the word "sacrament."

The colonists were impatient of insulting actions as well as words. Sampson said in "Romeo and Juliet," "I will bite my thumb at them, which is a disgrace to them *if they bear it;*" so "finger-sticking" was a disgrace in colonial times *if unresented*, and it was actionable in the courts. The man or woman who pointed the finger of scorn at a neighbor was pretty sure to have the finger of the law pointed at him.

The curious practice of the Dutch settlers alluded to — the giving of nicknames — may be partly explained by the fact that in some cases the persons named had no surname, and the nickname was really a distinguishing name. These nicknames appear not only in the records of criminal cases, but in official documents such as the patents for towns, transfers of estates, civil contracts, etc. In Albany, in 1655 and 1657, we find Jan the Jester, Huybert the Rogue, Jacobus or Cobus the Looper, squint-eyed Harmen, the wicked Domine. On Long Island were John the Swede, Hans the Boor, Tunis the Fisher. In Harlem was Jan Archer the Koop-all (or buy-all). In New York, in English days, in 1691, we find Long Mary, Old Bush, Topknot Betty, Scarebouch. These names conveyed no offence, and seem to have been universally adopted and responded to.

It would appear to a casual observer glancing over the court-records of those early years of New York life under Dutch supremacy, that the greater number of the cases brought before the magistrates were these slander and libel cases. We could believe that no other court-room ever rang with such petty personal suits; to use Tennyson's words, "it bubbled o'er with gossip and scandal and spite." But in truth slander was severely punished in all the colonies, in New England, Virginia, Pennsylvania; and it is not to the detriment of the citizens of New Netherland that they were more sharp in the punishment of such offences, for it is well known, as Swift says, that the worthiest people are those most injured by slander.

The slander cases of colonial times seem most trivial and even absurd when seen through the mist of years. They could scarce reach the dignity of Piers Plowman's definition of slanders: —

"To bakbyten, and to bosten, and to bere fals witnesse
To scornie and to scolde, sclaundres to make."

To show their character, let me give those recorded in which Thomas Applegate of Gravesend, Long Island, took an accused part. In 1650, he was brought up before the Gravesend court for saying of a fellow-townsman that "he thought if his debts were paid he would have little left." For this incautious but not very heinous speech he paid a fine of forty guilders. The next year we find him prosecuted for saying of a neighbor that "he had not half a wife." Though he at first denied this speech, he was ordered "to make publick acknowledgement of error; to stand at the publick post with a paper on his breast mentioning the reason, that he is a notorious, scandalous person." This brought him to his senses, and he confessed his guilt, desired the slandered "half a wife" to "pass it by and remit it, which she freely did and he gave her thanks." Next Mistress Applegate was brought up for saying that a neighbor's wife milked the Applegate cows. She escaped punishment by proving that Penelope Prince told her so. As a climax, Thomas Applegate said to a friend that he believed that the Governor took bribes. The *schout* in his decision on this grave offence said Applegate "did deserve to have his tongue bored through with a hot iron;" but this fierce punishment was not awarded him, nor was he banished.

When the tailor of New Amsterdam said disrespectful words of the Governor, his sentence was that he "stand before the Governor's door with uncovered head, after the ringing of the bell, and to declare that he falsely and scandalously issued such words and then to ask God's pardon."

The magistrates were very touchy of their dignity. Poor Widow Piertje Jans had her house sold on an execution; and, exasperated by the proceeding, and apparently also at the price obtained, she said bitterly to the officers, "Ye despoilers, ye bloodsuckers, ye have not sold but given away my house." Instead of treating these as the heated words of a disappointed and unhappy woman, the officers promptly ran tattling to the Stadt Huys and whiningly complained to the Court that her words were "a sting which could not be endured." Piertje was in turn called shameful; her words were termed "foul, villanous, injurious, nay, infamous words," and also called a blasphemy, insult, affront, and reproach. She was accused of insulting, defaming, affronting, and reproaching the Court, and that she was in the highest degree reprimanded, particularly corrected, and severely punished; and after being forbidden to indulge in any more such blasphemies, she was released, — "bethumped with words," as Shakespeare said, — doubtless well scared at the enormity of her offence, as well as at the enormity of the magistrate's phraseology.

The notary Walewyn van der Veen was frequently in trouble, usually for contempt of court. And I doubt not "the little bench of justices" was sometimes rather trying in its ways to a notary who knew anything about law. On one occasion, when a case relating to a bill of exchange had been decided against him, Van der Veen spoke of their High Mightinesses the magistrates as "simpletons and blockheads." This was the scathing sentence of his punishment: —

"That Walewyn Van der Veen, for his committed insult, shall here beg forgiveness, with uncovered head, of God, Justice, and the Worshipful Court, and moreover pay as a fine 190 guilders."

This fine must have consumed all his fees for many a weary month thereafter, if we can judge by the meagre lawyers' bills which have come down to us.

Another time the contumacious Van der Veen called the Secretary a rascal. Thereat, the latter, much aggrieved, demanded "honorable and profitable reparation" for the insult. The *schout* judged this epithet to be a slander and an affront to the Secretary, which "affected his honor, being tender," and the honor of the Court as well, since it was to a member of the Court, and he demanded that the notary should pay a fine of fifty guilders as an example to other slanderers, "who for trifles have constantly in their mouths curses and abuses of other honorable people."

Another well-known notary and practitioner and pleader in the busy little Court held in the Stadt Huys was Solomon La Chair. His manuscript volume of nearly three hundred pages, containing detailed accounts of all the business he transacted in Manhattan, is now in the County Clerk's Office in New York, and proves valuable material for the historiographer. He had much business, for he could speak and write both English and Dutch; and he was a faithful, painstaking, intelligent worker. He not only conducted lawsuits for others, but he seems to have been in constant legal hot water himself on his own account. He was sued for drinking and not paying for a can of sugared wine; and also for a half-aam of costly French wine; and he was sued for the balance of payment for a house he had purchased; he pleaded for more time, and with the ingenuous guilelessness peculiar to the law said in explanation that he had had the money gathered at one time for payment, but it had somehow dropped through his fingers. "The Court condemned to pay at once," — not being taken in by any such simplicity as that. He had to pay a fine of twelve guilders for affronting both fire inspector and court messenger. He first insulted the *brandt-meester* who came to inspect his chimney, and was fined, then he called the *bode* who came to collect the fine "a little cock booted and spurred." The Court in sentence said with dignity, "It is not meet that men should mock and scoff at persons appointed to any office, yea a necessary office."

He won one important suit for the town of Gravesend, by which the right of that town to the entire region of Coney Island was established; and he received in payment for his legal services therein, the munificent sum of twenty-four florins (ten dollars) paid in gray pease. He kept a tavern and was complained of for tapping after nine o'clock; and he was sued by his landlord for rent; and he had a yacht, "The Pear Tree," which ran on trading trips to Albany, and there were two or three lawsuits in regard to that. He was also a farmer of the excise on slaughtered cattle; but, in spite of all his energy and variety of employment, he died insolvent in 1664. The last lawsuit in which Lawyer Solomon had any share was through a posthumous connection, — the burgher who furnished an anker of French wine for the notary's funeral claimed a position as preferred creditor to the estate.

A very aggravated case of scorn and resistance of authority was that of Abel Hardenbrock against the *schout* de Mill. And this case shows equally the popular horror of violations of the law and the confiding trust of the justices that the word of the law was enough without any visible restraining force. Hardenbrock, who was a troublesome fellow, had behaved most vilely, shoving the *schout* on the breast, and wickedly "wishing the devil might break his neck," simply because the *schout* went to Hardenbrock's house to warn his wife not to annoy further Burgomaster De Peyster by unwelcome visits. Hardenbrock was accordingly seized and made a prisoner at the Stadt Huys " in the chamber of Pieter Schaefbanck, where he carried on and made a racket like one possessed and mad, notwithstanding the efforts of Heer Burgomaster Van Brught, running up to the Court room and going away next morning as if he had not been imprisoned." It was said with amusing simplicity that this cool walking out of prison was " contrary to the customs of the law," and a fine of twenty-five florins was imposed.

For serious words against the government, which could be regarded as treasonable, the decreed punishment was death. One Claerbout van ter Goes used such words (unfortunately they are not given in the indictment), and a judgment was recorded from each burgomaster and *schepen* as to what punishment would be proper. He was branded, whipped on a half-gallows, and banished, and escaped hanging only by one vote.

All classes in the community were parties in these petty slander suits; schoolmasters and parsons appear to have been specially active. Domine Bogardus and Domine Schaets had many a slander suit. The most famous and amusing of all these clerical suits is the one brought by Domine Bogardus and his wife, the posthumously famous Anneke Jans, against Grietje von Salee, a woman of very dingy reputation, who told in New Amsterdam that the domine's wife, Mistress Anneke, had lifted her petticoats in unseemly and extreme fashion when crossing a muddy street. This was proved to be false, and the evidence adduced was so destructive of Grietje's character that she stands disgraced forever in history as the worst woman in New Netherland.

Not only were slanderers punished, but they were disgraced with terrible names. William Bakker was called "a blasphemer, a street schold, a murderer as far as his intentions are concerned, a defamer, a disturber of public peace," — the concentration of which must have made William Bakker hang his head in the place of his banishment. They were also rebuked from the pulpit, and admonished in private.

Perhaps the best rebuke given, as well as a

unique one, was the one adopted by Domine Frelinghuysen, who had suffered somewhat from slander himself. He had this rhyme painted in large letters on the back of his sleigh, that he who followed might read: —

"Niemands tong; nog neimands pen,
Maakt my anders dan ik ben.
Spreek quaad-spreekers: spreek vonder end,
Niemand en word van u geschend."

Which, translated into English, reads: —

"No one's tongue, and no one's pen
Makes me other than I am.
Speak, evil-speakers, speak without end,
No one heeds a word you say."

The original Court of the colony was composed of a Director and his Council. In 1656, in answer to complaints from the colonists, the States-General ordered the election of a board of magistrates, in name and function like those of the Fatherland; namely, a *schout*, two burgomasters, and five *schepens*. The duties of the burgomasters and *schepens* were twofold: they regulated municipal affairs like a board of aldermen, and they sat as a court of justice both in civil and criminal cases. The annual salary of a burgomaster was fixed at one hundred and forty dollars, and of a *schepen* at one hundred dollars; but as these salaries were to come out of the municipal chest, which was chronically empty, they never were paid. When funds did come in from the excise on taverns, on slaughtered cattle, the tax on land, the fees on transfers, etc., it always had to be paid out in other ways, — for repairs for the school-room, the *Graft*, the watch-room, the Stadt Huys. It never entered the minds of those guileless civic rulers, two centuries ago, to pay themselves and let the other creditors go without. The early city *schout* was also *schout-fiskaal* till 1660; but the proper duties of this functionary were really a combination of those pertaining now to the mayor, sheriff, and district-attorney. In the little town one man could readily perform all these duties. He also presided in Court. An offender could thus be arrested, prosecuted, and judged, by one and the same person, which seems to us scarcely judicious; but the bench of magistrates had one useful power, that of mitigating and altering the sentence demanded by the *schout*. Often a fine of one hundred guilders would be reduced to twenty-five; often the order for whipping would be set aside, and the command of branding as well.

Sometimes justice in New York was tempered with mercy, and sorely it needed it when fierce English rule and law came in force. Felons were few, but these few were severely punished. A record of a trial in 1676 reveals a curious scene in Court, as well as an astonishing celerity in the execution of the law under English rule and in the English army. Three soldiers stole a couple of iron pots, two hoes, a pair of shears, and half a firkin of soap. They were tried in the morning, confessed, cast into "the Hole" in the afternoon, and in the evening "the Governor ordered some persons to go to the prisoners and advise them to prepare for another world, for that one of them should dye the next day." On the gloomy morrow, on Saturday, the three terror-stricken souls drew lots, and the fatal lot fell to one Thomas Weale. The court of aldermen interceded for him and finally secured his reprieve till Monday. The peaceful Dutch Sunday, darkened and shocked by this impending death, saw a strange and touching sight.

"In the evening a company of the chiefe women of the City, both English and Dutch, made earnest suite to the Governor for the Condemned man's life. Monday in the morning the same women who came the last night with many others of the better sort, and a greater number of the ordinary Dutch women, did again very much importune the Governor to spare him."

These tender-hearted colonists were indorsed and supplemented by the petition of Weale's fellow-soldiers in the garrison, who pleaded the prisoner's youth and his past usefulness, and who promised if he were pardoned never to steal nor to conceal theft. As a result of all this intercession, the Governor "graciously" granted pardon.

This promise and pardon seem to have accomplished much in army discipline, for thereafter arrests for crime among the soldiery were rare. Five years later a soldier was accused of pilfering.

"The Court Marshall doth adjudge that the said Melchoir Classen shall run the Gantlope once, the length of the fort: where according to the custome of that punishment, the souldiers shall have switches delivered to them, with which they shall strike him as he passes between them stript to the waist, and at the Fort-gate the Marshall is to receive him, and there to kick him out of the Garrison as a cashiered person, when he is no more to returne, and if any pay is due him it is to be forfeited."

And that was the end of Melchoir Classen.

Gantlope was the earlier and more correct form of the word now commonly called gantlet. Running the gantlope was a military punishment in universal use.

Another common punishment for soldiers (usually for rioting or drinking) was riding the wooden horse. In New Amsterdam the wooden horse stood between Paerel Street and the Fort, and was twelve feet high. Garret Segersen, for stealing chickens, rode the wooden horse for three days from two o'clock to close of parade with a fifty-pound weight tied to each foot. At other times a musket was tied to each foot of the disgraced man. One culprit rode with an empty scabbard in one hand and a pitcher in the other to show his inordinate love for John Barleycorn. Jan Alleman, a Dutch officer, challenged Jan de Fries, who was *bedridden;* for this cruel and meaningless insult he too rode the wooden horse. In Revolutionary days we still find the soldiers of the Continental Army punished by riding the wooden horse, or, as it was sometimes called, "the timber mare;" but it was probably a modification of the cruel punishment of the seventeenth century.

A sailor, for drawing a knife on a companion, was dropped three times from the yard-arm and received a kick from every sailor on the ship, — a form of running the gantlope. And we read of a woman who enlisted as a seaman, and whose sex was detected, being dropped three times from the yard-arm and tarred and feathered.

These women petitioners for Soldier Weale of whom I have told, were not the only tender-hearted New Yorkers to petition for " mercy, that herb of grace, to flower." During Stuyvesant's rule his sister, Madam Bayard, successfully interceded for the release, and thereby saved the life, of an imprisoned Quaker; and in September, 1713, two counterfeiters were saved from the death penalty by the intervention of New York dames. We read "Most of the gentlewomen of the city waited on the Governor, and addressed him earnestly with prayers and tears for the lives of the culprits, who were accordingly pardoned." When two sailors rioted through the town demanding food and drink, and used Carel Van Brugh so roughly that his face was cut, they were sentenced to be fastened to the whipping-post, and scourged, and have gashes cut in their faces; the wife of Van Brugh and her friends petitioned that the sentence should not be carried out, or at any rate executed within a room. Doubtless other examples could be found.

The laws of New Netherland were naturally based upon the laws and customs of the Fatherland, which in turn were formed by the rules of the College of XIX. from the Imperial Statutes of Charles V. and the Roman civil law.

The punishments were the ordinary ones of the times, neither more nor less severe than those of the Fatherland or the other colonies. In 1691 it was ordered that a ducking-stool be erected in New York on the wharf in front of the City Hall. The following year an order was passed that a pillory, cage, and ducking-stool be built. Though scolds were punished, I have never seen any sentence to show that this ducking-stool was ever built, or that one was ever used in New

York; while instances of the use of a ducking-stool are comparatively plentiful in the Southern colonies. The ducking-stool was an English "engine" of punishment, not a Dutch.

The colonists were astonishingly honest. Thieves were surprisingly few; they were punished under Dutch rule by scourging with rods, and usually by banishment, — a very convenient way of shifting responsibility. Assaults were punished by imprisonment and subjection to prison fare, consisting only of bread and water or *small beer;* and sometimes temporary banishment. There was at first no prison, so men were often imprisoned in their own houses, which does not seem very disgraceful. In the case of François de Bruyn, tried for insulting and striking the court messenger, he was fined two hundred guilders, and answered that he would rot in prison before he would pay. He was then ordered to be imprisoned *in a respectable tavern*, which sentence seems to have some possibility of mitigating accompaniments.

In 1692 it was ordered in Kings County that a good pair of stocks and a pound be made in every bound within Kings County, and kept in sufficient repair. In repair and in use were they kept till this century. Pillories too were employed in punishment till within the memory of persons now living. The whipping-post was really a public blessing, — in constant use, and apparently of constant benefit, though the publicity of its employment seems shocking to us to-day. The public whipper received a large salary. In 1751, we learn from an advertisement, it was twenty pounds annually.

Some of the punishments were really almost picturesque in their ingenious inventions of mortification and degradation. Truly it was a striking sight when "Jan of Leyden" — a foul-mouthed rogue, a true *blatherschuyten* — was fastened to a stake in front of the townhouse, with a bridle in his mouth and a bundle of rods tied under each arm, and a placard on his breast bearing the inscription, "Lampoon-riter, false accuser, defamer of magistrates." Though he was banished, I am sure he never was forgotten by the children who saw him standing thus garnished and branded on that spring day in 1664. In the same place a thief was punished by being forced to stand all day under a gallows, a gallows-rope around his neck and empty sword-scabbard in his hand, a memorable figure.

And could any who saw it ever forget the punishment of Mesaack Martens, who stole six cabbages from his neighbor, and confessed and stood for days in the pillory with cabbages on his head, that "the punishment might fit the crime;" to us also memorable because the prisoner was bootlessly *examined by torture* to force confession of stealing fowls, butter, turkeys, etc.

He was not the only poor creature who suffered torture in New Amsterdam. It was frequently threatened and several times executed. The mate of a ship was accused of assaulting a sheriff's officer, who could not identify positively his assailant. The poor mate was put to torture, and *he was innocent* of the offence. The assailant was proved to be another man from whom the officer had seized a keg of brandy. Still none in New Amsterdam were tortured or pressed to death. The blood of no Giles Corey stains the honor of New Netherland.

Sometimes the execution of justice seemed to "set a thief to catch a thief." A letter

COLONIAL DAYS

written by an English officer from Fort James on Manhattan Island to Captain Silvester Salisbury in Fort Albany in 1672 contains this sentence: —

"We had like to have lost our Hang-man Ben Johnson, for he being taken in Divers Thefts and Robbings convicted and found guilty, escaped his neck through want of another Hangman to truss him up, soe that all the punishment that he received for his Three Years' Roguery in thieving and stealing (which was never found out till now) was only 39 stripes at the Whipping Post, loss of an Ear and Banishment."

We have the records of an attempt at capital punishment in 1641; and Mr. Gerard's account of it in his paper "The Old Stadt-Huys" is so graphic, I wish to give it in full: —

"The court proceedings before the Council, urged by the Fiscal, were against Jan of Fort Orange, Manuel Gerrit the Giant, Anthony Portugese, Simon Congo, and five others, all negroes belonging to the Company, for killing Jan Premero, another negro. The prisoners having pleaded guilty, and it being rather a costly operation to hang nine able-bodied negroes belonging to the Company, the sentence was that they were to draw lots to determine 'who should be punished with the cord until death, praying the Almighty God, the Creator of Heaven and Earth, to direct that the lot may fall on the guiltiest, whereupon' the record reads, 'the lot fell by God's Providence on *Manuel Gerrit, the Giant*, who was accordingly sentenced to be hanged by the neck until dead as an example to all such malefactors.' Four days after the trial, and on the day of the sentence, all *Nieuw Amsterdam* left its accustomed work to gaze on the unwonted spectacle. Various Indians also gathered, wondering, to the scene. The giant negro is brought out by the black hangman, and placed on the ladder against the fort with two strong halters around his neck. After an exhortation from Domine Bogardus during which the negro chaunts barbaric invocations to his favorite Fetich, he is duly turned off the ladder into the air. Under the violent struggles and weight of the giant, however, both halters break. He falls to the ground. He utters piteous cries. Now on his knees, now twisting and groveling on the earth. The women shriek. The men join in his prayers for mercy to the stern Director. He is no trifler and the law must have its course. The hangman prepares a stronger rope. Finally the cry for mercy is so general that the Director relents, and the fortunate giant is led off the ground by his swarthy friends, somewhat disturbed in his intellect by his near view of the grim King of Terrors."

Up to February 21, 1788, benefit of clergy existed; that is, the plea in capital felonies of being able to read. This was a monkish privilege first extended only to priestly persons. In England it was not abolished till 1827. The minutes of the Court of General Quarter Sessions in New York bear records of criminals who pleaded "the benefit" and were branded on the brawn of the left thumb with "T" in open court and then discharged.

As the punishments accorded for crimes were not severe for the notions of the times, it is almost amusing to read some fierce ordinances, — though there is no record of any executions in accordance with them. For instance, in January, 1659, by the Director-General and Council with the advice of the burgomasters and *schepens* it was enacted that "No person shall strip the fences of posts or rails under penalty for the first offence of being whipped and branded, and for the second, of punishment with the cord until death ensues." It is really astonishing to think of these kindly Dutch gentlemen calmly ordering hanging for stealing fence-rails, though of course the matter reached further than at first appeared: there was danger of a scarcity of grain; and if the fences were stolen, the cattle would trample down and destroy the grain. Later orders as to fences were given which appear eminently calculated to be mischief-making. " Persons thinking their neighbors' fences not good, first to request them to repair; failing which to report to the overseers." In 1674 all persons were forbidden to leave the city except by city-gate, under penalty of death; this was of course when war threatened.

The crime of suicide was not without punishment. Suicides were denied ordinary burial rites. In Dutch days when one Smitt of New York committed suicide, the *schout* asked that his body be drawn on a hurdle and buried with a stake in his heart. This order was not executed; he was buried at night and his estates confiscated. When Sir Danvers Osborne — the Governor for a day — was found dead by his own act, he was " decently interred in Trinity churchyard."

Women in New York sometimes made their appearance in New York courts, as in those of other colonies, in another rôle than that of witness or criminal; they sometimes sat on juries. In the year 1701, six good Albany wives served on a jury: Tryntje

Roseboom, Catheren Gysbertse, Angeneutt Jacobse, Marritje Dirkse, Elsje Lansing, and Susanna Bratt. They were, of course, empanelled for a special duty, not to serve on the entire evidence of the case for which they were engaged.

Many old records are found which employ quaint metaphors or legal expressions; I give one which refers to a custom which seems at one time to have been literally performed. It occurs in a commission granted to the trustees of an estate of which the debts exceeded the assets. Any widow in Holland or New Netherland could be relieved of all demands or claims of her husband's creditors by relinquishing all right of inheritance. This widow took this privilege; it is recorded thus: —

"*Whereas*, Harman Jacobsen Bamboes has been lately shot dead, murdered by the Indians, and whereas the estate left by him *has been kicked away with the foot by his wife who has laid the key on the coffin*, it is therefore necessary to authorize and qualify some persons to regulate the same."

There was a well-known Dutch saying which referred to this privilege, *Den Sleutel op het graf leggen*, and simply meant not to pay the debts of the deceased.

This legal term and custom is of ancient origin. In Davies' "History of Holland" we read of a similar form being gone through with in Holland in 1404, according to the law of Rhynland. The widow of a great nobleman immediately after his death desired to renounce all claim on his estate and responsibility for his debts. She chose a guardian, and, advancing with him to the door of the Court (where the body of the dead Count had been placed on a bier), announced that she was dressed wholly in borrowed clothing; she then formally gave a straw to her guardian, who threw it on the dead body, saying he renounced for her all right of dower, and abjured all debts. This was derived from a still more ancient custom of the Franks, who renounced all alliances by the symbolic breaking and throwing away a straw.

In other states of the Netherlands the widow gave up dower and debts by laying a key and purse on the coffin. This immunity was claimed by persons in high rank, one being the widow of the Count of Flanders.

In New England (as I have told at length

in my book, "Customs and Fashions in Old New England," the widow who wished to renounce her husband's debts was married in her shift, often at the cross-roads, at midnight. These shift-marriages took place in Massachusetts as late as 1836; I have a copy of a court record of that date.

I know of but one instance of the odious and degrading English custom of wife-trading taking place in New York. Laurens Duyts, an agent for Anneke Jans in some of her business transactions, was in the year 1663 sentenced to be flogged and have his right ear cut off for selling his wife, Mistress Duyts, to one Jansen. Possibly the severity of the punishment may have prevented the recurrence of the crime.

After a somewhat extended study and comparison of the early court and church records of New England with those of New York, I cannot fail to draw the conclusion — if it is just to judge from such comparisons — that the state of social morals was higher in the Dutch colonies than in the English. Perhaps the settlers of Boston and Plymouth were more severe towards suspicion of immorality, as they were infinitely more severe towards suspicion of irreligion, than were their Dutch neighbors. And they may have given more publicity and punishment to deviations from the path of rectitude and uprightness; but certainly from their own records no fair-minded person can fail to deem them more frail, more erring, more wicked, than the Dutch. The circumstances of immigration and the tendencies of temperament were diverse, and perhaps it was natural that a reaction tending to sin and vice should come to the intense and overwrought religionist rather than to the phlegmatic and prosperous trader. In Virginia and Maryland the presence of many convict-emigrants would form a reasonable basis for the existence of the crime and law-breaking which certainly was in those colonies far in excess of the crime in New Netherland and New York.

I know that Rev. Mr. Miller, the English clergyman, did not give the settlement a very good name at the last of the seventeenth century; but even his strictures cannot force me to believe the colonists so unbearably wicked.

It should also be emphasized that New Netherland was far more tolerant, more generous than New England to all of differing religious faiths. Under Stuyvesant, however, Quakers were interdicted from preaching, were banished, and one Friend was treated with great cruelty. The Dutch clergymen opposed the establishment of a Lutheran church, and were rebuked by the Directors in Holland, who said that in the future they would send out clergymen " not tainted with any needless preciseness;" and Stuyvesant was also rebuked for issuing an ordinance imposing a penalty for holding conventicles not in accordance with the Synod of Dort. Many Christians not in accordance in belief with that synod settled in New Netherland. Quakers, Lutherans, Church of England folk, Anabaptists, Huguenots, Waldenses, Walloons. The Jews were protected and admitted to the rights of citizenship. Director Kieft, with heavy ransoms, rescued the captive Jesuits, Father Jogues and Father Bressani, from the Indians and tenderly cared for them. No witches suffered death in New York, and no statute law existed against witchcraft. There is record of but one witchcraft trial under the English governor, Nicholls, who speedily joined with the Dutch in setting aside all that nonsense.

CHAPTER XIII

CHURCH AND SUNDAY IN OLD NEW YORK

SUNDAY was not observed in New Netherland with any such rigidity as in New England. The followers of Cocceius would not willingly include Saturday night, and not even all of the Sabbath day, in their holy time. Madam Knight, writing in 1704 of a visit to New York, noted: "The Dutch are n't strict in keeping the Sabbath as in Boston and other places where I have been." This was, of course, in times of English rule in New York. Still, much respect to the day was required, especially under the governing hand of the rigid Calvinist Stuyvesant. He specially enjoined and enforced strict regard for seemly quiet during service time. The records of Stuyvesant's government are full of injunctions and laws prohibiting "tavern-tapping" during the hours of church service. He would not tolerate fishing, gathering of berries or nuts, playing in the street, nor gaming at ball or bowls during church time. At a little later date the time of prohibition of noise and tapping and gaming was extended to include the entire Sabbath day, and the *schout*, was ordered to be active in searching out and punishing such offenders.

Occasionally his vigilance did discover some Sabbath disorders. He found the first Jew trader who came to the island of Manhattan serenely keeping open shop on Sunday, and selling during sermon time, knowing naught of any Sunday laws of New Amsterdam.

And Albert the Trumpeter was seen on the Sabbath in suspicious guise, with an axe on his shoulder, — but he was only going to cut a bat for his little son; and as for his neighbor who did cut wood, it was only kindling, since his children were cold.

And one Sunday evening in 1660 the *schout* triumphantly found three sailors round a taphouse table with a lighted candle and a backgammon-board thereon; and he surely had a right to draw an inference of gaming therefrom.

And in another public-house ninepins were

visible, and a can and glass, during preaching-time. The landlady had *her* excuse, — some came to her house and said church was out, and one chanced to have a bowl in his hand and another a pin, but there was no playing at bowls.

Still, though he snooped and fined, in 1656 the burgomasters learned " by daily and painful experience" that the profanation of " the Lord's day of Rest by the dangerous, Yes, damnable Sale or Dealing out of Wines Beers and Brandy-Waters" still went on; and fresh Sunday Laws were issued forbidding "the ordinary and customary Labors of callings, such as Sowing, Mowing, Building, Sawing wood, Smithing, Bleeching, Hunting, Fishing." All idle sports were banned and named: "Dancing, Card-playing, Tick-tacking, Playing at ball, at bowls, at ninepins; taking Jaunts in Boats, Wagons, or Carriages."

In 1673, again, the magistrates " experienced to our great grief" that rolling ninepins was more in vogue on Sunday than on any other day. And we learn that there were social clubs that " Set on the Sabbath," which must speedily be put an end to.

COLONIAL DAYS

Thirty men were found by the *schout* in one *tap-huys;* but as they were playing ninepins and backgammon two hours after the church-doors had closed, prosecution was most reluctantly abandoned.

Of course scores of "tappers" were prosecuted, both in taverns and private houses. Piety and regard for an orderly Sabbath were not the only guiding thoughts in the burgomasters' minds in framing these Sunday liquor laws and enforcing them; for some tapsters had "tapped beer during divine service and used a small kind of measure which is in contempt of our religion and must ruin our state," — and the state was sacred. In the country, as for instance on Long Island, the carting of grain, travelling for pleasure, and shooting of wild-fowl on Sunday were duly punished in the local courts.

I do not think that children were as rigid church attendants in New York as in New England. In 1696, in Albany, we find this injunction: "ye Constables in eache warde to take thought in attending at ye church to hender such children as Profane ye Sabbath;" and we know that Albany boys and girls were complained of for coasting down hill on

Sunday, — which enormity would have been simply impossible in New England, except in an isolated outburst of Adamic depravity. In another New York town the "Athoatys" complained of the violation of the Sabbath by "the Younger Sort of people in Discourssing of Vane things and Running of Raesses." As for the city of New York, even at Revolutionary times a cage was set up on City Hall Park in which to confine wicked New York boys who profaned the Sabbath. I do not find so full provisions made for seating children in Dutch Reformed churches as in Puritan meeting-houses. A wise saying of Martin Luther's was "Public sermons do very little edify children" — perhaps the Dutch agreed with him. As the children were taught the Bible and the catechism every day in the week, their spiritual and religious schooling was sufficient without the Sunday sermon, — but, of course, if they were not in the church during services, they would "talk of vane Things and run Raesses."

Before the arrival of any Dutch preacher in the new settlement in the new world, the spiritual care of the little company was provided for by men appointed to a benign and beautiful old Dutch office, and called *krankebesoeckers* or *zeikentroosters*, — "comforters of the Sick," — who not only tenderly comforted the sick and weary of heart, but "read to the Commonalty on Sundays from texts of Scripture with the Comments." These pious men were assigned to this godly work in Fort Orange and in New Amsterdam and Breuckelen. In Esopus they had meetings every Sunday, "and one among us read something for a postille." Often special books of sermons were read to the congregations.

In Fort Orange they had a domine before they had a church. The patroon instructed Van Curler to build a church in 1642; but it was not until 1646 that the little wooden edifice was really put up. It was furnished at a cost of about thirty-two dollars by carpenter Fredricksen, with a *predickstoel*, or pulpit, a seat for the magistrates, — *de Heerebanke*, — one for the deacons, nine benches and several corner-seats.

The first church at Albany, built in 1657, was simply a block house with loop-holes for the convenient use of guns in defence against the Indians, — if defence were needed. On the roof were placed three small cannon commanding the three roads which led to it. This edifice was called "a handsome preaching-house," and its congregation boasted that it was almost as large as the fine new one in New Amsterdam. Its corner-stone was laid with much ceremony. In its belfry hung a bell presented to the little congregation by the Directors of the Amsterdam Chamber of the West India Company. The *predickstoel* was the gift of the same board of West India Directors, since the twenty-five beavers' skins sent for its purchase proved greatly damaged, and hence inadequate as payment.

This pulpit still exists, — a pedestal with a flight of narrow steps and curved balustrade. It is about four feet in height to its floor, and only three in diameter. It is octagonal; one of the sides is hinged, and forms the entrance door or gate. All the small trimmings and mouldings are of oak, and it has a small bracket or frame to hold the hour-glass. It stood in a space at the end of the centre aisle.

> "I see the pulpit high — an octagon,
> Its pedestal, doophuysje, winding stair,
> And room within for one, and one alone,
> A canopy above, suspended there."

COLONIAL DAYS

From the ceiling hung a chandelier, and candle-sconces projected from the walls. There were originally two low-set galleries; a third was added in 1682. The men sat in the galleries, and as they carried their arms to meeting, were thus conveniently placed to fire through the loop-holes if necessity arose. The bell-rope from the belfry hung down in the middle of the church, and when not in use was twisted round a post set for the purpose.

This church was plain enough, but it was certainly kept in true Dutch cleanliness, for house-cleaners frequently invaded it with pails and scrubbing-brushes, brooms, lime, and sand. Even the chandelier was scoured, and a *ragebol*, or cobweb-brush, was purchased by the deacon for the use of the scrubbers. The floor was sanded with fine beach-sand, as were the floors of dwelling-houses. I find in the records of the Long Island churches frequent entries of payments for church brooms and church sand, — in Jamaica as late a date as 1836. In 1841 the deacons bought a carpet.

In 1715 the second Albany church was built, on the site of the old one. As Pepys tells of St. Paul's of London, so tradition says this Albany church was built around the first one, that the congregation were only three weeks deprived of the use of the church, and the old one was carried out " by piece meal." At any rate, it was precisely similar in shape, but was a substantial edifice of stone. This building was not demolished until 1806.

The sittings in this church sold for thirty shillings each, and were, as it was termed, "booked to next of kin." When the first owner of a seat died (were he a man), the seat descended to his son or the eldest of his grandsons; if there was no son nor grandson, to his son-in-law; this heir being in default, the sitting fell to a brother, and so on. When the transfer was made, the successor paid fifteen shillings to the church. A woman's seat descended to her daughter, daughter-in-law, or sister. Sittings were sold only to persons residing in Albany County. When a seat was not claimed by any heir of a former owner, it reverted to the church.

This church had some pretence to ornamentation. The windows were of stained glass decorated with the coat-of-arms of various Albany families. The panes with the Van Renssellaer and Dudley arms are still in existence. Painted escutcheons also hung on the walls, as they did in the church in Garden Street, New York. This was a custom of the Fatherland. A writer of that day said of the church in Harlem, "It is battered as full of scutcheons as the walls can hold."

The meeting-house sometimes bore other decorations,—often "Billets of sales," and notices of vendues or "outcrys." Lost swine and empounded swine were signified by placards; town meetings and laws were posted. In the Albany church, when there was rumor of an approaching war with France, "powder, bales," and guns to the number of fifty were ordered to be "hung up in ye church,"—a stern reminder of possible sudden bloodshed. "Y^e fyre-masters" were also ordered to see that "ye fyre-ladders and fyre-hooks were hung at ye church."

In 1698 a stone church was built in Flatbush. It cost nearly sixteen thousand guilders. It had a steep four-sided roof, ending in the centre in a small steeple. This roof was badly constructed, for it pressed out the upper part of one wall more than a foot over the foundation, and sorely bent the braces. The pulpit faced the door, and was flanked by the deacons' bench on one side and the elders' bench on the other.

Of the seating arrangement of this Flatbush church Dr. Strong says:—

"The male part of the congregation were seated in a continuous pew all along the wall, divided into twenty apartments, with a sufficient number of doors for entrance, each person having one or more seats. The residue of the interior of the building was for the accommodation of the female part of the congregation, who were seated on chairs. These were arranged into seven rows or blocks, and every family had one or more chairs in some one of these blocks. This arrangement of seats was called ' De Gestoeltens.' Each chair was marked on the back by a number or by the name of the person to whom it belonged."

When the church was remodelled, in 1774, there were two galleries, one for white folk, one for black; the benches directly under the galleries were free. In the centre of the main floor were two benches with backs, one called the Yefrows Bench, the other the Blue Bench. The former was for the minister's wife and family; the other was let out to individuals, and was a seat of considerable dignity.

COLONIAL DAYS

Many of the old Dutch churches, especially those on Long Island, were six-sided or eight-sided; these had always a high, steep, pyramidal roof terminating in a belfry, which was often topped by a gilded *weerhaen*, or weathercock. The churches at Jamaica and New Utrecht were octagonal. The Bushwick church was hexagonal. It stood till 1827,—a little, dingy, rustic edifice. This form of architecture was not peculiar to the Dutch nor to the Dutch Reformed Church. Episcopal churches and the Quaker meeting-house at Flushing were similar in shape.

When the bold sea-captain De Vries, that interesting figure in the early history of New Netherland, arrived in churchless New Amsterdam, he promptly rallied Director Kieft on his dilatoriness and ungodliness, saying it was a shame to let Englishmen see the mean barn which served Manhattan as a church; and he drew odious comparisons,—that "the first thing they build in New England after their dwelling-houses is a fine church." He pointed out the abundant materials for building creditably and cheaply,—fine oak wood, good mountain stone, excellent lime; and he did more,—he supported his advice by a subscription of a hundred guilders. Director Kieft promised a thousand guilders from the West India Company; and Fortune favored the scheme, for the daughter of Domine Bogardus was married opportunely just at that time; and as has been told in Chapter III., according to the wise custom of the day in Holland, and consequently in America, a collection was taken up at the wedding. Kieft asked that it be employed for the building of a church; and soon a stone church seventy-two feet long and fifty-five feet wide was erected within the Fort. It was the finest building in New Netherland, and bore on its face a stone inscribed with these words: "Anno Domini 1641, William Kieft, Director-General, hath the Commonalty built this Temple." It was used by the congregation as a church for fifty years, and for half a century longer by the military as a post-building, when it was burned.

There was no church in Breuckelen in 1660. Domine Selyns wrote, "We preach in a barn." The church was built six years later, and is described as square, with thick stone walls and steep peaked roof surmounted by a small open belfry, in which hung the small, sharp-toned bell which had been sent over as a gift by the West India Company. The walls were so panelled with dark wood, the windows were so high and narrow, that it was always dark and gloomy within; even in summer-time it was impossible to see to read in it after four o'clock in the afternoon. Services were held in summer at 9 A. M. and 2 P. M., and in the winter in the morning only. The windows were eight feet from the floor, and were darkened with stained glass sent from Holland, representing flower-pots with vines covered with vari-colored flowers. This church stood in the middle of the road on what is now Fulton Street, a mile from the ferry, and was used until 1810.

These early churches were unheated, and it is told that the half-frozen domines preached with heavy knit or fur caps pulled over their ears, and wearing mittens, or *wollen handt-schoenen;* and that *myn heer* as well as *myn vrouw* carried muffs. It is easy to fancy some men carrying muffs,— some love-locked Cavalier or mincing Horace Walpole; but such feminine gear seems to consort ill with an Albany Dutchman. That he should light his long pipe in meeting was natural enough, — to keep warm; though folk do say that he smoked in meeting in summer too, — to keep cool. By the middle of the eighteenth century the Albany and Schenectady churches had stoves perched up on pillars on a level with the gallery, — in high disregard or ignorance of the laws of calorics; hence, of course, the galleries, in which sat the men, were fairly heated, while the ground floor and the *vrouws* remained below in icy frigidity. It is told of more than one old-time sexton, that he loudly asserted his office and his importance by noisy rattling-down and replenishing of the gallery stoves and slamming of the iron doors at the most critical point in the domine's sermon. Cornelius Van Schaick, the Albany sexton, made his triumphant way to the stoves, slashing with his switch (perhaps his dog-whip) all the boys who chanced to be in his way.

The women of the congregation carried foot-stoves of perforated metal or wood, which were filled with a box of living coals, to afford a little warmth to the feet. Many now living remember the scratching sound of these stoves on the boards or the sanded floor as they were passed from warm feet to cold feet near at hand. *Kerck-stooven* appear on the earliest inventories, were used in America until our own day, and still are used in the churches in Holland. In an anteroom in a Leyden church may be seen several hundred *stooven* for use in the winter.

It is stated of the churches in New York City that until 1802 services were held, even in the winter-time, with wide-open doors, and that often the snow lay in little drifts up the aisles,— which may have been one reason why young folk flocked to Trinity Church.

One very handsome church-equipment of the women attendants of the Dutch Reformed church was the Psalm-book. This was usually bound with the New Testament; and both were often mounted and clasped with silver. Sometimes they had two silver rings at the back through which ribbons could be passed, to hang thereby the books on the back of a chair if desired. Sometimes the books had silver chains. Rarely they were mounted in gold. The inventory of the estate of nearly every well-to-do Dutch woman, resident of New York, Albany, or the larger towns, shows one, and sometimes half-a-dozen of these silver-mounted Psalm-books. Elizabeth Van Es had two Bibles with silver clasps, two Psalm-books, and two Catechisms. These books were somewhat dingily printed, in old Dutch, on coarse but durable paper; the music was on every page beside the words. The notes of music were square, heavily printed, rough-hewn, angular notes,—"like stones in the walls of a churchyard," says Longfellow of the Psalm-book of the Pilgrims. The metrical version of the Psalms was simple and impressive, and is certainly better literary work in Dutch than is the Bay Psalm-book in English.

The services in these churches were long. They were opened by reading and singing conducted by the *voorleezer* or *voorzanger*, — that general-utility man who was usually precentor, schoolmaster, bell-ringer, sexton, grave-digger, and often town-clerk. As ordered by the Assembly of XIX., in 1645, he "tuned the psalm;" and during the first singing the domine entered, and, pausing for a few moments, sometimes kneeling at the foot of the pulpit-stairs, in silent prayer, he soon ascended to his platform of state. The psalms were given out to the congregation through the medium of a large hanging-board with movable printed slips, and this was in the charge of the *voorleezer*. Of course the powers of this church functionary varied in different towns. In all he seems to have had charge of the turning of the hour-glass which stood near the pulpit in sight of the domine. In Kingston, where the pulpit was high, he thrust up to the preacher the notices stuck in the end of a cleft stick. In this town, at the time of the Revolution, he was also paid two shillings per annum by each family to go around and knock loudly on the door each Sunday morning to warn that it was service-time. In some towns he was permitted to give three sharp raps of warning with his staff on the pulpit when the hour-glass had run out a second time, — thus shutting off the sermon. The *voorleezer* is scarcely an obsolete church-officer to-day. In 1865 died the last Albany *voorleezer*, and the Flatbush *voorleezer* is well remembered and beloved.

The clerk in New Amsterdam was a marked personage on Sunday. After he had summoned the congregation by the sound of drum or bell, he ceremoniously formed a pompous little procession of his underlings, and, heading the line, he carried with their assistance the cushions from the City Hall to the church, to furnish comfortably the "Magistrate's Pew," in which the burgomasters and *schepens* sat.

The deacons had full control of all the funds of the church; they collected the contributions of the congregation by walking up and down the aisles and thrusting in front of each "range" of seats in the face of the seated people small cloth contribution-bags, or *sacjes*, hung on a hoop at the end of a slender pole six or eight feet in length, — fashioned, in fact, somewhat after the model of scoop-nets. This custom — the use of so unfamiliar a medium for church-collecting — gave rise to the amusing notion of one observant English traveller that Dutch deacons passed round their old hats on the end of a walking-stick to gather church-contributions.

Often a little bell hung at the bottom of the contribution-bag, or was concealed in an ornamenting tassel, and by its suggestive tinkle-tinkle warned all church-attendants of the approach of the deacon, and perhaps aroused the peaceful church-sleepers from too selfish dreams of profitable barter in peltries. In New Utrecht the church *sacje* had an alarm-bell which sounded only when a contribution was made. A loud-speaking silence betrayed the stingy church-goer. The collection was usually taken up in the middle of a sermon. The *sacjes* stood or hung conveniently in the deacon's seat. In Flatbush and other towns the deacons paused for a time in front of the pulpit — *sacje* in hand — while the domine enjoined generosity to the church and kindly Christian thought of the poor. The collection-bags in Flatbush were of velvet.

It is said that stray Indians who chanced to wander or were piously persuaded to enter into the Fort Orange or Albany church during service-time, and who did not well understand the pulpit eloquence of the Dutch tongue, regarded with suspicious and disapproving eyes the unfailing and unreasonable appearance of the *karck-sacje;* for they plainly perceived that there was some occult law of cause and effect which could be deduced from these two facts, — the traders who gave freely into the church-bags on Sunday always beat down the price of beaver on Monday.

IN OLD NEW YORK

The bill for one of these *karck-sacjes* was paid by the deacons of the Albany church in 1682. Seven guilders were given for the black stuff and two skeins of silk, and two guilders for the making. When a ring was bought for the sack (I suppose to hold it open at the top), it cost four guilders. This instrument of church-collection lingered long in isolated localities. It is vaguely related that some *karck-sacjes* are still in existence and still used. The church at New Utrecht possessed and exhibited theirs at their bicentennial celebration a few years ago. The fate of the *sacje* was decreed when the honest deacons were forced to conclude that it could, if artfully manipulated by designing moderns, conceal far too well the amount given by each contributor, and equally well concealed the many and heavy stones deposited therein by vain youth of Dutch descent but American ungodliness. So an open-faced full-in-view pewter or silver plate was substituted and passed in its place. In 1813 the church at Success, Long Island, bought contribution plates and abandoned the *sacje*. Some lovers of the good old times resented this inevitable exposure of the amount of each gift, and turned away from the deacon and his innovating fashion and refused to give at all.

I ought to add, in defence of the *karcksacjes*, and in praise of the early congregations, that the amount gathered each week was most generous, and in proportion far in advance of our modern church-contributions. The poor were not taken charge of by state or town, but were liberally cared for in each community by its church; occasionally, however, assistance was given through the assignment to the church by the courts of a portion of the money paid as fines in civil and criminal cases. In New York a deacon's house with nurses resident, took the place of an almshouse.

Often during the year much more money was collected than was needful for the current expenses of the church. In Albany the extra collections were lent out at eight per cent interest; at one time four thousand guilders were lent to one man. The deacons who took charge of the treasury chest in Albany each year rendered an account of its contents. In 1665 there were in this chest *seelver-gelt, sea-want,* and *obligasse,* or obligations, to the amount of 2829 guilders.

IN OLD NEW YORK

In 1667 there were 3299 guilders; also good Friesland stockings and many ells of linen to be given to the poor.

In some churches poor-boxes were placed at the door. The Garden Street Church in New York had two strong boxes bound with iron, with a small hole in the padlocked lid, and painted with the figure of a beggar leaning on a staff,— which, according to the testimony of travellers, was a sight unknown in reality in New York at that time.

The "church-poor," as they were called, fared well in New Netherland. Of degraded poor of Dutch birth or descent there were none. Some poor folk, and old or sickly, having a little property, transferred it to the Consistory, who paid it out as long as it lasted, and cheerfully added to the amount by gifts from the church-treasury as long as was necessary for the support of those "of the poorer sort." To show that these church-poor were neither neglected nor despised, let me give one example of a case — an ordinary one — from the deacons' records of the Albany church in 1695. Claes Janse was assigned at that time to live with Hans Kros and his wife Antje. They were to provide him with *logement, kost, drank, wassen* (lodging, food, drink, and washing), and for this were paid forty guilders a month by the church. When Claes died, the church paid for his funeral, which apparently left nothing undone in the way of respectability. The bill reads thus:—

Dead shirt and cap . . 16 guilders.		
Winding sheet . . . 14 "		
Making coffin . . . 24 "		
1 lb. nails, cartage coffin 3 "	10 stuyvers.	
2 Half Vats good beer . 30 "		
6 bottles Rum . . . 22 "		
5 gallons Madeira Wine 42 "		
Tobacco, pipes, and sugar 4 "	10	"
3 cartloads sand for grave 1 "	10	"
Gravedigging . . . . 3 "		

Deacons give three dry boards for coffin and use of pall.

With a good dry coffin, a good dry grave, and a far from dry funeral, Hans Claes' days, though he were of the church-poor, ended in honor.

The earlier Dutch ministers were some of them rather rough characters. Domine Bogardus, in New Amsterdam, and Domine Schaets, in Fort Orange, were most unclerical in demeanor, both in and out of the pulpit. Both were engaged in slander suits, the former as libeller and defendant; both were abusive and personal in the pulpit, "dishonoring the church by passion." The former was alleged by his enemies to be frequently drunk, in church and abroad; and, fearless of authority, he seized the pulpit as a convenient and prominent platform from which he could denounce his opposers. From his high post he scolded the magistrates, called opprobrious names (a hateful offence in New Amsterdam), threatened Wouter Van Twiller that he would give "from the pulpit such a shake as would make him shudder." He even arbitrarily refused the Communion, thereby causing constant scandal and dissension. The magistrates doubtless deserved all his rebukes, but in their written admonition to him they appear with some dignity, expressing themselves forcibly and concisely thus: "Your bad tongue is the cause of these divisions, and your obstinacy the cause of their continuance;" and it is difficult now to assign the blame and odium of this quarrel very decidedly to either party.

The domine did not have everything his

own way on Sundays, for the Director drowned his vociferations by ordering the beating of drums and firing of cannon outside the church during services; and denounced the sermons in picturesque language as "the rattling of old wives' stories drawn out from a distaff."

The Labadist travellers thus described the Albany domine: —

"We went to church in the morning [April 28, 1680], and heard Domine Schaets preach, who, although he is a poor old ignorant person, and besides is not of good life, yet had to give utterance to his passion, having for his text 'Whatever is taken upon us,' etc., at which many of his auditors, who knew us better, were not well pleased, and in order to show their condemnation of it, laughed and derided him, which we corrected."

In turn the Lutheran minister was dubbed by the Dutch domines "a rolling, rollicking, unseemly carl, more inclined to pore over the wine-kan than to look into the Bible." And we all know what both Lutherans and Dutch thought of the Quaker preachers; so all denominations appear equally rude.

The salaries of the ministers were liberal even in early days; that of Domine Megapolensis (the second minister sent to New

Netherland) was, I think, a very fair one. He agreed to remain in the colony six years, and was given free passage for himself and family to the new world; an outfit of three hundred guilders; a salary of three hundred guilders a year for three years, and five hundred annually during the three remaining years; and an annual tithe of thirty schepels of wheat and two firkins of butter. If he died before the term expired, his wife was to have a pension of a hundred guilders a year for the unexpired term. The first revenue relinquished by the West India Company to the town of New Amsterdam was the "tapster's excise,"—the excise on wine, beer, and spirits,—and the sole condition made by Stuyvesant on its surrender, as to its application, was that the salaries of the two domines should be paid from it.

As time passed on, firewood became one of the minister's perquisites, in addition to his salary, sixty or seventy loads a season. We find the Schenectady congregation having a "bee" to gather in the domine's wood; and the Consistory supplied plentiful wine, rum, and beer as a treat for the "bee."

What Cotton Mather called the "angelical

conjunction" of piety and physic sometimes was found in the person of the ministers of the Dutch Reformed church, but not so constantly as among the Puritan ministers. Domine Rubel, sent out by the Classis of Amsterdam, was settled over the churches in Kings County. He was more devoted to the preparation of quack medicines than to the saving of souls. One of his advertisements of March 28, 1778, reads thus:—

> "It has pleased Almighty God to give me the wisdom to find out the *Golden Mother Tincture* and such a Universal Pill as will cure most diseases. I have studied European physicians in four different languages. I don't take much money as I want no more than a small living whereto God will give his blessing.
> JOHANNES CASPARUS RUBEL, Minister of the Gospel and Chymicus."

This does not let us wonder that after a while his parish became dissatisfied with his ministrations, and that he ended his days in dishonor.

The employment of the Dutch language in the pulpit in New York churches lasted until into this century. Naturally, Dutch was used as long as the Classis at Amsterdam supplied the churches in America with preachers. In 1744 Domine Rubel and Domine Van Sinderin were sent to Flatbush, the last ministers sent from the Classis of Amsterdam to any American church; but at their death the Dutch tongue was not silent in the Flatbush church; for their successor, Domine Schoonmaker, lived to be ninety years old, and never preached but one sermon in English. With his death, in 1824, ceased the public use of the Dutch language in the Flatbush pulpit. Until the year 1792 the entire service in his church was " the gospel undefiled, in Holland Dutch." Until the year 1830 services in the sequestered churches in the Catskills were held alternately in Dutch and English. Until 1777 all the records of the Sleepy Hollow church were kept in Dutch; and in 1785 all its services were in Dutch. In September of that year, a little child, Lovine Hauws, was baptized in English by the new minister, Rev. Stephen Van Voorhees. This raised a small Dutch tempest, and the new domine soon left that parish.

In New York City the large English immigration, the constant requirements and influences of commerce, and the frequent intermarriages of the English and Dutch robbed the Dutch language of its predominance by the middle of the eighteenth century. Rev. Dr. Laidlie preached in 1764 the first English sermon to a Dutch Reformed congregation. By 1773 English was used in the Dutch school, and young people began to shun the Dutch services.

The growth of the Dutch Reformed church in New York was slow; this was owing to three marked and direct causes: —

First, from 1693 until Revolutionary times Episcopacy was virtually established by law in a large part of the province, — in the city and county of New York, and in the counties of Westchester, Richmond, and Queens; and though the Dutch Reformed church was protected and respected, people of all denominations were obliged to contribute to the support of the Episcopal church.

Second, the English language had become the current language of the province; in the schools, the courts, in all public business it was the prevailing tongue, while the services of the Dutch Reformed church were by preference held in Dutch.

IN OLD NEW YORK

Third, all candidates for ministry in the Dutch Reformed church were obliged to go to Holland for ordination; this was a great expense, and often kept congregations without a minister for a long time. The entire discipline of the church — all the Courts of Appeal — was also in the Fatherland.

In order to obtain relief from the last-named hampering condition, a few ministers in America devised a plan, in 1737, to secure church-organization in New York. It took the slow-moving Classis of Amsterdam ten years to signify approval of this plan, and a body was formed, named the Cœtus. But this had merely advisory powers, and in less than ten years it asked to be constituted a Classis with full ecclesiastical powers. From this step arose a violent and bitter quarrel, which lasted fifteen years, — until 1771, — between the Cœtus party, the Reformers, and the Conferentie party, the Conservatives. The permission of the Classis of Amsterdam for American church independence was finally given on condition of establishing a college for the proper training of the ministry of the Dutch Reformed church. The Cœtus party obtained a charter from George III. for a college, which, called Queens College, was blighted in its birth by the Revolution, but lived with varying prosperity until its successful revival, under the name of Rutgers College, in 1825.

CHAPTER XIV

"THE END OF HIS DAYS"

As soon as a death had been announced to the dwellers in any little town in colonial New York, by the slow ringing or tolling of the church-bell, there went forth solemnly from his home the *aanspreecker*, or funeral-inviter (who might be grave-digger, bell-ringer, schoolmaster, or chorister, and who was usually all four), attired in gloomy black, with hat fluttering long streamers of crape; and with much punctilio he visited all the relatives and friends of the deceased person, notified them of the death, advised them of the day and hour of the funeral, and requested their honorable presence. This inviting was a matter of most rigid etiquette; no one in these Dutch-American communities of slightest dignity or regard for social proprieties would attend a funeral unbidden. The *aanspreecker* was paid at regular rates for his service as living perambulating obituary notice, according to the distance travelled and the time spent, if he lived in a country town where distances between houses were great.

In 1691 the " inviters to the buryiall of deceased persons" in New York were public officers, appointed and licensed by the Mayor. Their names were Conradus Vanderbeck and Richard Chapman, and they were bidden to give their attendance gratis to the poor. A law was passed in New York in 1731, setting the fees of " inviters to funerals " at eighteen shillings for the funeral of any one over twenty years of age; for a person between twelve and twenty years, twelve shillings; for one under twelve years, eight shillings. For a large circle of friends these sums seem small. The Flatbush inviter in 1682 had twelve guilders for inviting to the funeral of a grown person, and only four guilders in addition if he invited in New York, — which was poor pay enough, when we think of the long ride and the row across. In 1760 we find the New York inviter, Evert Fels, advertising his change of residence, and that he can be found if needed next King's Stores. It is easy to imagine that the *aanspreecker* must have been a somewhat self-important personage, who doubtless soberly enjoyed his profession of mortuary news-purveyor, and who must have been greeted wherever he went with that grewsome interest which in colonial days attached to everything pertaining to death.

This public officer and custom was probably derived from the Romans, who used to send a public crier about, inviting the people to the solemnization of a funeral. In the northern counties of England each village had its regular "bidder," who announced his "funeral-bidding" by knocking on each door with a great key. Sometimes he "cried" the funeral through the town with a hand-bell. In New York the fashion was purely of Dutch derivation. In Holland the *aanspreecker* was an official appointed by government, and authorized to invite for the funerals of persons of all faiths and denominations who chanced to die in his parish.

In New York, ever bent on fashions new, the *aanspreecker*, on mournful mission intent, no longer walks our city avenues nor even our country lanes or village streets; but in Holland he still is a familiar form. Not, as of old, the honored schoolmaster, but simply a hired servant of the undertaker, he rushes with haste through the streets of Dutch towns. Still clad in dingy black of ancient fashion, kneebreeches, buckled shoes, long cloak, cocked hat with long streamers of crape, he seems the sombre ghost of old-time manners. Sometimes he bears written invitations deep bordered with black; sometimes he calls the death and time of funeral, as did the Roman *præco;* and sometimes, with streamers of white, and white cockade on his hat, he goes on a kindred duty, — he bears to a circle of friends or relatives the news of a birth.

Before the burial took place, in olden times, a number of persons, usually intimate friends of the dead, watched the body throughout the night. Liberally supplied with various bodily comforts, such as abundant strong drink, plentiful tobacco and pipes, and newly baked cakes, these watchers were not wholly gloomy, nor did the midnight hours lag unsolaced. The great *kamer* in which the body lay, the state-room of the house, was an apartment so rarely used on other occasions than a funeral that in many households it was known as the *doed-kamer*, or dead-room.

Sometimes it had a separate front door by which it was entered, thus giving two front doors to the house. Diedrich Knickerbocker says the front door of New York houses was never opened save for funerals, New Years, and such holidays. The kitchen door certainly offered a more cheerful welcome. In North Holland the custom still exists of reserving a room with separate outside entrance, for use for weddings and funerals. Hence the common saying in Holland that doors are not made for going in and out of the house.

Men and women both served as watchers, and sometimes both were at the funeral services within the *doed-kamer;* but when the body was borne to the grave on the wooden bier resting on the shoulders of the chosen bearers, it was followed by men only. The women remained for a time in the house where the funeral had taken place, and ate *doed-koecks* and sipped Madeira wine.

The coffin, made of well-seasoned boards, was often covered with black cloth. Over it was spread the *docd-kleed*, a pall of fringed black cloth. This *doed-kleed* was the property of the church, as was the pall in New England churches, and was usually stored with the bier in the church-vestibule, or *doop-huys*. In case of a death in childbirth, a heavy white sheet took the place of the black pall. This practice also obtained in Yorkshire, England.

Among the Dutch a funeral was a most costly function. The expenditure upon funeral gloves, scarfs, and rings, which was universal in New England, was augmented in New York by the gift of a bottle of wine and a linen scarf.

When Philip Livingstone died, in 1749, his funeral was held both in New York and at the Manor. He had lived in Broad Street, and the lower rooms of his house and those of his neighbors were thrown open to receive the assemblage. A pipe of wine was spiced for the guests, and the eight bearers were each given a pair of gloves, a mourning-ring, a scarf, handkerchief, and a monkey-spoon. At the Manor a similar ceremony took place, and a pair of gloves and handkerchief were given to each tenant. The whole expense was five hundred pounds. When Madam Livingstone died, we find her son writing to New York from the Manor for a piece of black Strouds to cover the four hearse-horses;

for a "Barrell of Cutt Tobacco and Long Pipes of which I am out;" for six silver tankards and cinnamon for the burnt wine; he said he had bottles, decanters, and glasses enough. The expense of these funerals may have been the inspiration for William Livingstone's paper on extravagance in funerals.

A monkey-spoon was a handsome piece of silver bearing the figure or head of an ape on the handle. *Mannetiens* spoons, also used in New Netherland, were similar in design. At the funeral of Henry De Forest, an early resident of New Harlem in 1637, his bearers were given spoons.

A familiar and extreme example of excess at funerals as told by Judge Egbert Benson was at the obsequies of Lucas Wyngaard, an old bachelor who died in Albany in 1756. The attendance was very large, and after the burial a large number of the friends of the dead man returned to the house, and literally made a night of it. These sober Albany citizens drank up a pipe of wine, and smoked many pounds of tobacco. They broke hundreds of pipes and all the decanters and glasses in the house, and wound up by burning all their funeral scarfs in a heap in the fireplace.

In Albany the expense, as well as the rioting, of funerals seems to have reached a climax. It is said that the obsequies of the first wife of Hon. Stephen Van Rensselaer cost twenty thousand dollars. Two thousand linen scarfs were given, and all the tenants were entertained for several days.

On Long Island every young man of good family began in his youth to lay aside money in gold coin to pay for his funeral; and a superior stock of wine was also saved for the same occasion. In Albany the cask of choice Madeira which was bought for a wedding and used in part, was saved in remainder for the funeral of the bridegroom.

The honor of a lavish funeral was not given to the wealthy and great and distinguished only. The close of every life, no matter how humble, how unsuccessful, was through the dignity conferred by death afforded a triumphal exit by the medium of "a fine burying."

In the preceding chapter the funeral of a penniless Albanian is noted; in 1696 Ryseck Swart also became one of the church-poor of Albany. She was not wholly penniless; she had a little silver and a few petty jewels, and a little strip of pasture land, worth in all about three hundred guilders. These she transferred to the church, for the Consistory to take charge of and dole out to her. A good soul, Marritje Lievertse, was from that time paid by the church thirty-six guilders a month for caring for Ryseck. I do not doubt she had tender care, for she was the last of the real church-poor (soon they had paupers and an almshouse), and she lived four years, and cost the parish two thousand two hundred and twenty-nine guilders. She died on February 15, 1700, and, though a pauper, she departed this life neither unwept, unhonored, nor unsung. Had she been the cherished wife of a burgomaster or *schepen*, she could scarce have had a more fully rounded or more proper funeral. The bill, which was paid by the church, was as follows: —

	g.	s.
3 dry boards for a coffin	7	10
¾ lb. nails	1	10
Making coffin	24	
Cartage	10	

	g.
Half a vat and an anker of good beer	27
1 gallon Rum	21
6 gallons Madeira for women and men	84
Sugar and *cruyery*	5
150 Sugar cakes	15
Tobacco and pipes	5
Grave digger	30
Use of pall	10
Wife Jans Lockermans	36
	232 guilders.

Rosenboom, for many years the *voor-leeser* and *dood-graver* and *aanspreecker* in Albany, sent in a bill of twelve guilders for delivering invitations to the funeral,—which bill was rejected by the deacons as exorbitant. But the invitations were delivered just the same, for even colonial paupers had friends, and her coffin was not made of green wood held together with wooden pegs, which some poor bodies had to endure; and the one hundred and fifty *doed-koecks* 'and Madeira for the women very evenly balanced the plentiful beer and wine and tobacco for the men. Truly, to quote one of Dyckman's letters from Albany, "the poor's purse here was richly garnisht."

An account of Albany, written by a traveller thereto in 1789, showed the continued existence of these funeral customs. It runs thus: —

"Their funeral customs are equally singular. None attend them without a previous invitation. At the appointed hour they meet at the neighboring houses or stoops until the corpse is brought out. Ten or twelve persons are appointed to take the bier altogether, and are not relieved. The clerk then desires the gentlemen (for ladies never walk to the grave, nor even attend the funeral unless a near relation) to fall into the procession. They go to the grave and return to the house of mourning in the same order. Here the tables are handsomely set and furnished with cold and spiced wine, tobacco and pipes, and candles, paper, etc., to light them. The house of mourning is soon converted into a house of feasting."

In New York we find old citizens leaving directions in their wills that their funeral shall be conducted in "the old Dutch fashion," not liking the comparatively simpler modern modes.

The customs were nearly the same in English families. At the funeral of Hon. Rufus King at Jamaica, Long Island, in 1827, which was held upon an exceptionally hot day in April, silver salvers holding decanters of wine and spirits, glasses and cigars, were constantly passed, both indoors and out, where many stood waiting the bearing of the coffin to the grave.

The transition of the funeral customs of ante-Revolutionary days into those of our own may partially be learned from this account written in 1858 by Rev. Peter Van Pelt, telling Domine Schoonmaker's method of conducting a funeral in the year 1819:

"The deceased had, many years before, provided and laid away the materials for his own coffin. This one was of the best seasoned and smoothest boards and beautifully grained. As I entered the room I observed the coffin elevated on a table in one corner. The Domine, abstracted and grave, was seated at the upper end; and around in solemn silence, the venerable and hoary-headed friends of the deceased. A simple recognition or a half-audible inquiry as one after another arrived was all that passed. Directly the sexton, followed by a servant, made his appearance with glasses and decanters. Wine was handed to each. Some declined; others drank a solitary glass. This ended, again the sexton presented himself with pipes and tobacco. The Domine smoked his pipe and a few followed his example. The custom has become obsolete, and it is well that it has. When the whiffs of smoke had ceased to curl around the head of the Domine, he arose with evident feeling, and in a quiet subdued tone, made a short but apparently impressive address. I judged solely by his appearance and manner; for although boasting a Holland descent, it was to me an unknown tongue. A short prayer concluded the service; and then the sexton taking the lead, followed the Domine, doctor, and pallbearers with white scarfs and black gloves. The corpse and long procession of friends and neighbors proceeded to the churchyard."

Not only were materials for the coffin secured and made ready during the lifetime, but often a shroud was made and kept for use. Instances have been known where a shroud was laid by unused for so many years that it became too yellow and discolored to use at all, and was replaced by another. Sometimes a new unlaundered shirt was laid aside for years to use as a *doed-hemde*. Two curious superstitions were rife in some localities, especially on Long Island; one was the careful covering of all the mirrors in the house, from the time of the death till after the funeral; the other the pathetically picturesque "telling the bees." Whittier's gentle rhyme on the subject has made familiar to modern readers the custom of " telling the bees of one, gone on the journey we all must go."

Both an English and Dutch funeral fashion was the serving to the attendants of the funeral of funeral-cakes. In New York and New Netherland these were a distinctive kind of *koeckje* known as *doed-koecks*, literally dead-cakes. An old receipt for their manufacture is thus given by Mrs. Ferris: " Fourteen pounds of flour, six pounds of sugar, five pounds of butter, one quart of water, two teaspoonfuls of pearlash, two teaspoonfuls of salt, one ounce of Caraway seed. Cut in thick dishes four inches in diameter." They were, therefore, in substance much like our New Year's cakes. Sometimes they were marked with the initials of the deceased person; and often they were carried home and kept for years as a memento of the dead, — perhaps of the pleasures of the funeral. One baker in Albany made a specialty of these cakes, but often they were baked at home. Sometimes two of these *doed-koecks* were sent with a bottle of wine and a pair of gloves as a summons to the funeral.

In Whitby, England, a similar cake is still made by bakers and served at funerals; but it is sprinkled with white sugar. In Lincolnshire and Cumberland like customs still exist. "Burial-cakes" were advertised by a baker in 1748 in the Philadelphia newspapers.

It is frequently asserted that funeral rings were commonly given among the Dutch. It seems fair to infer that more of them would have been in existence to-day if the custom had been universal. Scores of them can be found in New England. There is an enamelled ring marked "K. V. R., obit Sept. 16, 1719," which was given at the funeral of Kileaen Van Renssalaer. One of the Earl of Bellomont is also known, and two in the Lefferts family, dating towards the close of the past century. I have heard of a few others in Hudson Valley towns. Perhaps with gifts of gloves, spoons, bottles of wine, *doed-koecks*, scarfs, or handkerchiefs, rings would have been superfluous.

It will be noted in all these references to funerals herein given that the services were held in private houses; it was not until almost our own day that the funerals of those of Dutch descent were held in the churches.

COLONIAL DAYS

Interments were made under the churches; and, by special payment, a church-attendant could be buried under the seat in which he was wont to sit during his lifetime. The cost of interment in the Flatbush church was two pounds for the body of a child under six years; three pounds for a person from six to sixteen years of age; four pounds for an adult; and in addition "those who are inclined to be permitted to be interred in the church are required to pay the expense of every person." I don't know exactly what this ambiguous sentence can mean, but it was at any rate an extra charge "for the profit of the schoolmaster," who dug the grave and carried the dirt out of the church, and was paid twenty-seven guilders for this sexton's work for an adult, and less for a younger person and hence a smaller grave. Usually the domines were buried in front of the pulpit where they had stood so often in life.

After newspaper-days arrived in the colony, there blossomed in print scores of long death-notices, thoroughly in the taste of the day, but not to our taste. In the "New York Gazette" of December 24, 1750, we find a characteristic one: —

IN OLD NEW YORK

"Last Friday Morning departed this Life after a lingering Illness the Honorable Mrs. Roddam, wife to Robert Roddam, Esq. Commander of his Majesty's Ship Greyhound, now on this Station, and eldest Daughter of his Excellency our Governor. We hear she is to be Interred this Evening.

"Good Mr. Parker — Dont let the Character of our Deceased Friend, Mrs. Roddam, slip through your Fingers, as that of her Person through those of the Doctors. That she was a most affable and perfectly Good-Natured young Lady, with Good Sense and Politeness is well known to all her Acquaintances, and became one of the most affectionate Wives.

> "Immatura peri, sed tu felicior, Annos
> Vivi mens, Conjux optime, vive tuos

were the Sentiments of her Later Moments when I had the Honour to attend her. As this is intended as a small Tribute to the Manes of my dear departed Friend, your inserting of it will oblige one of your constant Female Readers and Humble Servant."

Another, of a well-known colonial dame, reads thus : —

"Last Monday died in the 80th year of her Age, and on Thursday was decently interred in the Family Vault at Morrisania : Isabella Morris, Widow and Relict of his Excellency Lewis Morris, Esq., Late Governor of the Province of New Jersey: A Lady endowed with every Qualification Requisite to render the Sex agreeable and entertaining, through all the Various scenes of Life. She was a pattern of Conjugal Affection, a tender Parent, a sincere Friend, and an excellent Oeconomist.

> She was
> Liberal, without Prodigality
> Frugal, without Parsimony
> Chearful, without Levity
> Exalted, without Pride.
> In person, Amiable
> In conversation, Affable
> In friendship, Faithful
> Of Envy, void.

She passed through Life endow'd with every Grace
Her virtues! Black Detraction can't deface;
Or Cruel Envy e'er eclipse her Fame;
Nor Mouldering Time obliterate her Name."

The tiresome, pompous, verbose productions, Johnsonian in phrase and fulsome in sentiment, which effloresced on the death of any man in public life or of great wealth, need not be repeated here. They were monotonously devoid of imagination and originality, being full of idle repetitions from each other, and whoever has labored through one can judge of them all.

IN OLD NEW YORK

It does not give us a very exalted notion of the sincerity or value of these funeral testimonials, or the mental capacity of our ancestors, to read in the newspapers advertisements of printed circulars of praise for the dead, eulogistic in every aspect of the life of the departed, and suitable for various ages and either sex, to be filled in with the name of the deceased, his late residence, and date of death.

Puttenham in the "Arte of English Poesie," says: "An Epitaph is an inscription such as a man may commodiously write or engrave vpon a tombe in few verses, pithie, quicke, and sententious, for the passer-by to peruse and judge vpon without any long tariaunce."

There need be no "long tariaunce" for either inquisitive or irreverent search over the tombstones of the Dutch, for the dignified and simple inscriptions are in marked contrast to the stilted affectations, the verbose enumerations, the pompous eulogies, which make many English "graveyard lines" a source of ridicule and a gratification of curiosity. Indeed, the Dutch inscriptions can scarcely be called epitaphs; the name, date of birth and death, are simply prefaced with the ever-recurring *Hier rust het lighaam*, Here rests the body; *Hier leydt het stoffelyk deel*, Here lie the earthly remains; or simpler still, *Hier leyt begraven*, Here lies buried. Sometimes is found the touching *Gedachtenis*, In remembrance. More impressive still, from its calm repetition on stone after stone, of an undying faith in a future life, are the ever-present words, *In den Heere ontslapen*, Sleeping in the Lord.

Not only in memory of those dead-and-gone colonists stand these simple Dutch tombstones, but in suggestive remembrance also of a language forever passed away from daily life in this land. The lichened lettering of those unfamiliar words seems in sombre truth the very voice of those honored dead who, in those green Dutch graveyards, in the shadow of the old Dutch churches, *in den Heere ontslapen*.